Runny Rainbows

Remarkable Creatures

A Stress-Relieving Coloring Book for Adults Featuring Majestic Animals, Mythical Creatures, Relaxing Mandalas, Beautiful Patterns and More

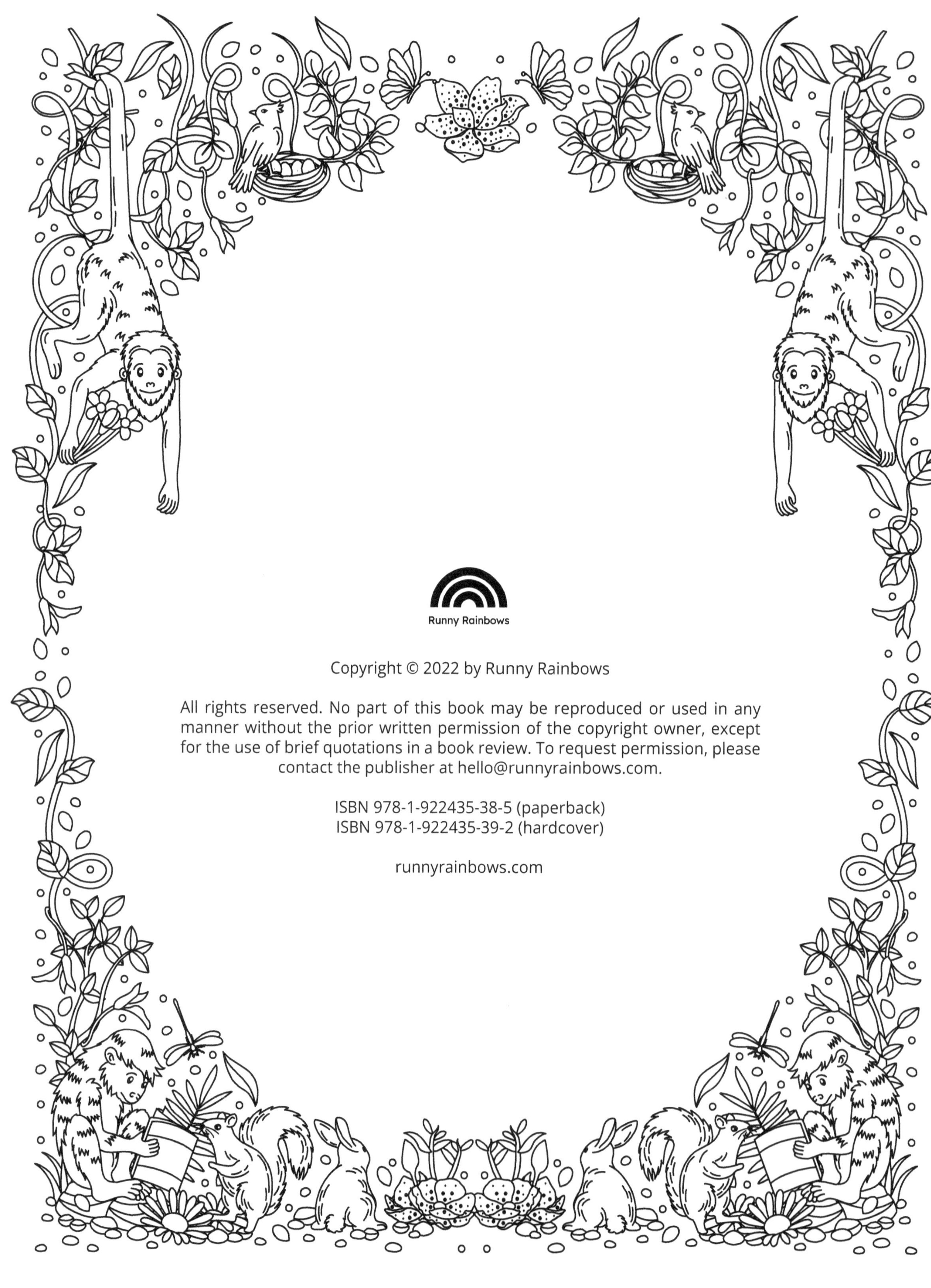

Runny Rainbows

ISBN 978-1-922435-38-5 (paperback)
ISBN 978-1-922435-39-2 (hardcover)

runnyrainbows.com

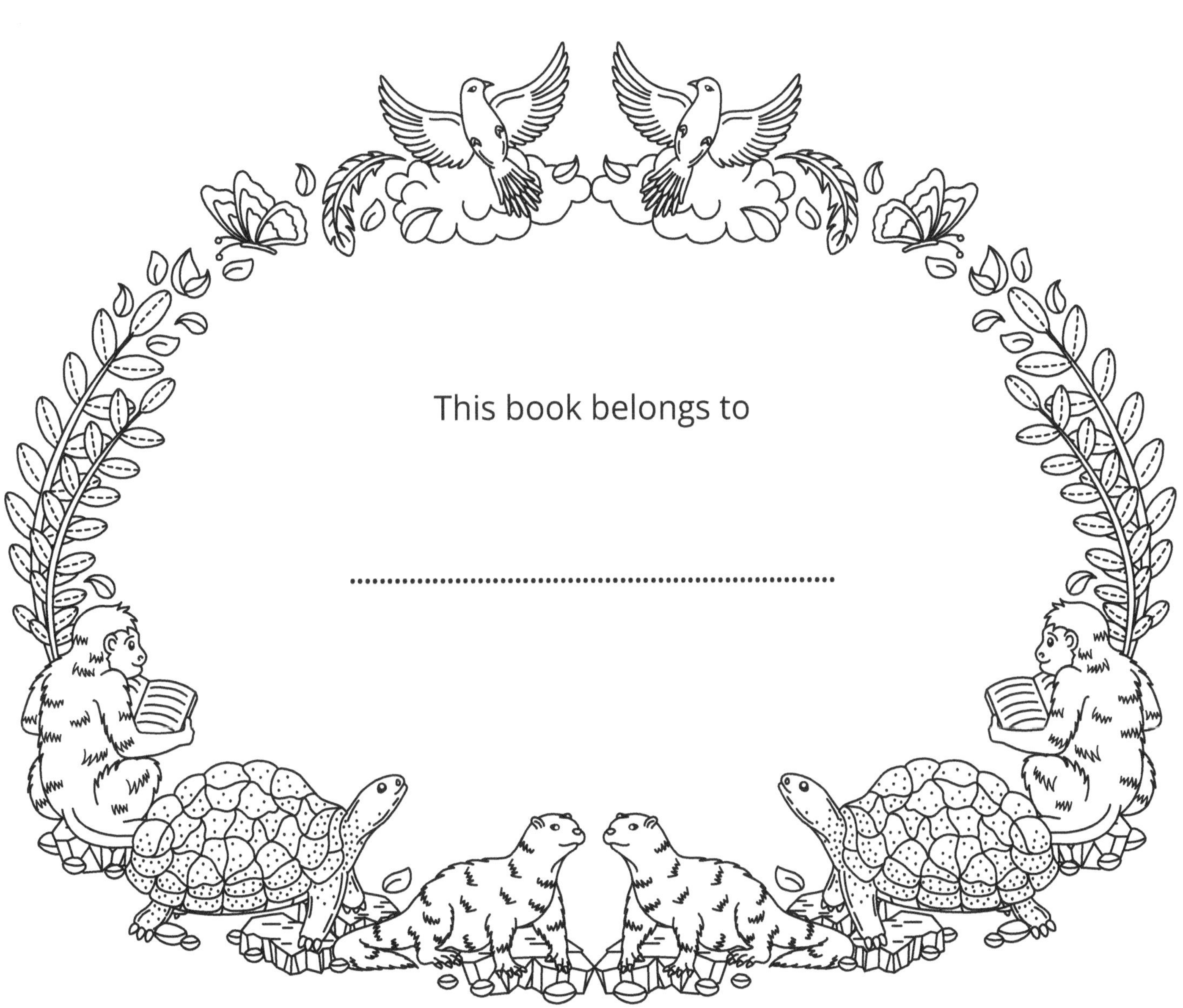

This book belongs to

....

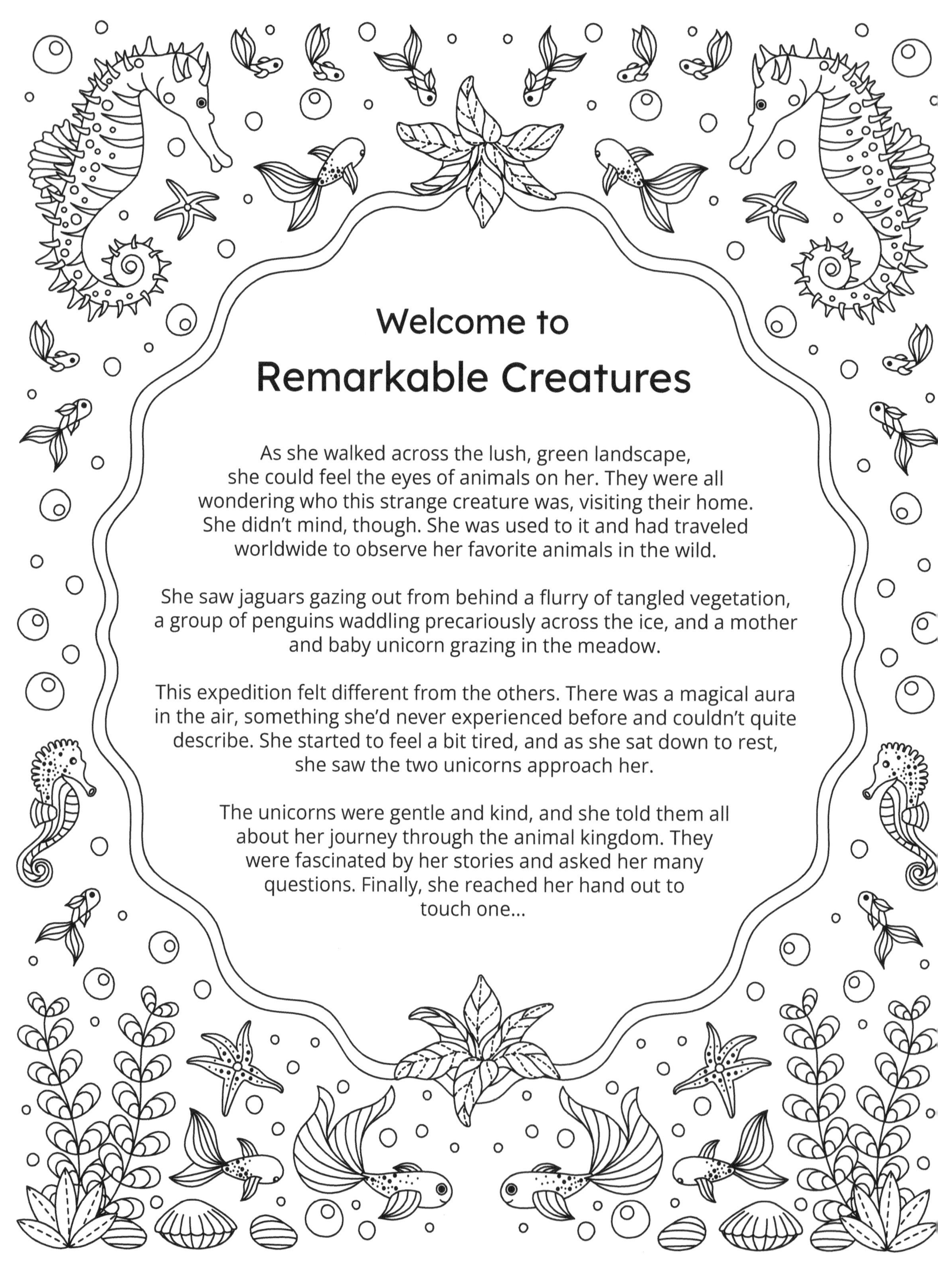

Welcome to
Remarkable Creatures

As she walked across the lush, green landscape,
she could feel the eyes of animals on her. They were all
wondering who this strange creature was, visiting their home.
She didn't mind, though. She was used to it and had traveled
worldwide to observe her favorite animals in the wild.

She saw jaguars gazing out from behind a flurry of tangled vegetation,
a group of penguins waddling precariously across the ice, and a mother
and baby unicorn grazing in the meadow.

This expedition felt different from the others. There was a magical aura
in the air, something she'd never experienced before and couldn't quite
describe. She started to feel a bit tired, and as she sat down to rest,
she saw the two unicorns approach her.

The unicorns were gentle and kind, and she told them all
about her journey through the animal kingdom. They
were fascinated by her stories and asked her many
questions. Finally, she reached her hand out to
touch one...

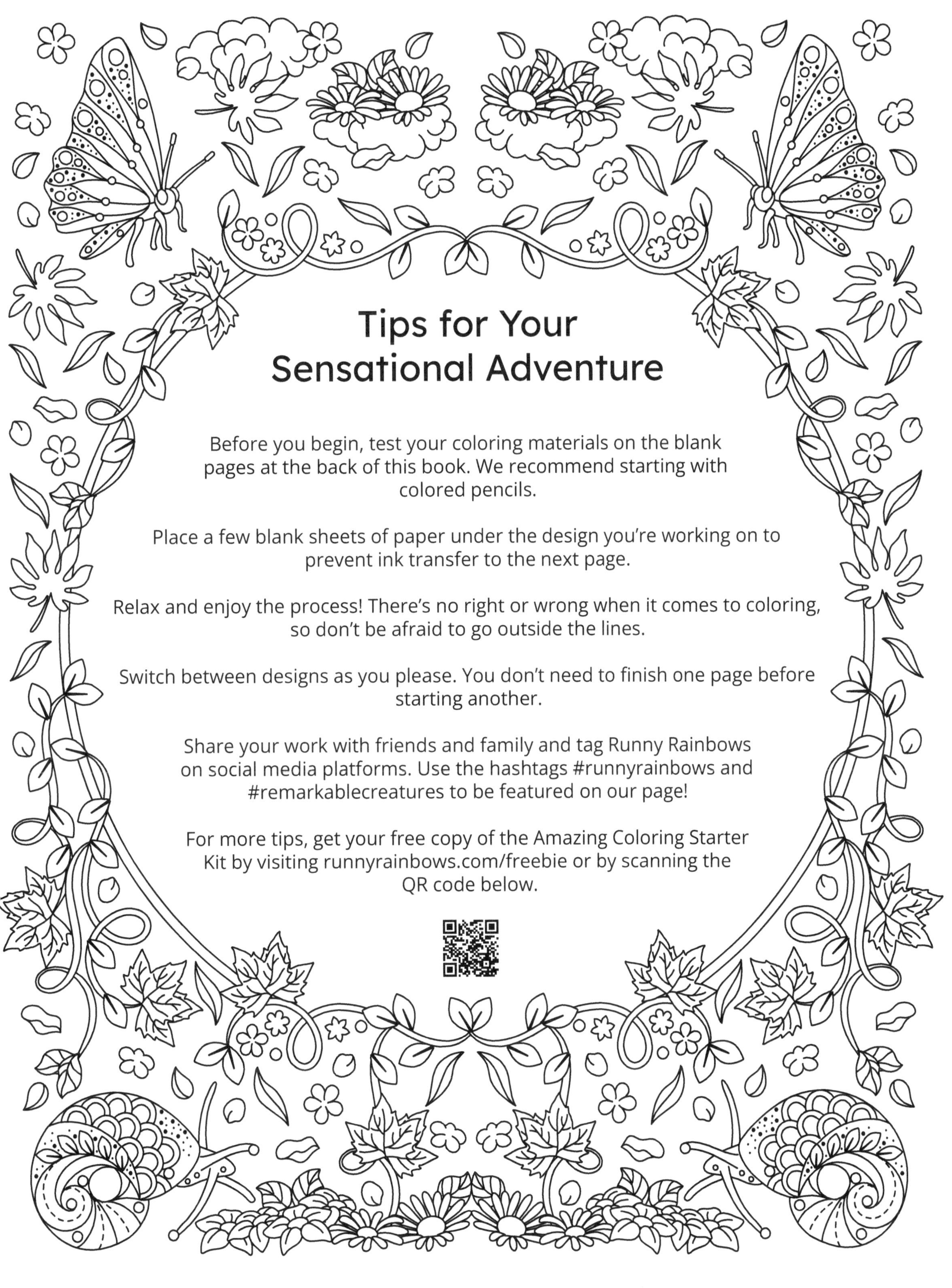

Tips for Your Sensational Adventure

Before you begin, test your coloring materials on the blank pages at the back of this book. We recommend starting with colored pencils.

Place a few blank sheets of paper under the design you're working on to prevent ink transfer to the next page.

Relax and enjoy the process! There's no right or wrong when it comes to coloring, so don't be afraid to go outside the lines.

Switch between designs as you please. You don't need to finish one page before starting another.

Share your work with friends and family and tag Runny Rainbows on social media platforms. Use the hashtags #runnyrainbows and #remarkablecreatures to be featured on our page!

For more tips, get your free copy of the Amazing Coloring Starter Kit by visiting runnyrainbows.com/freebie or by scanning the QR code below.

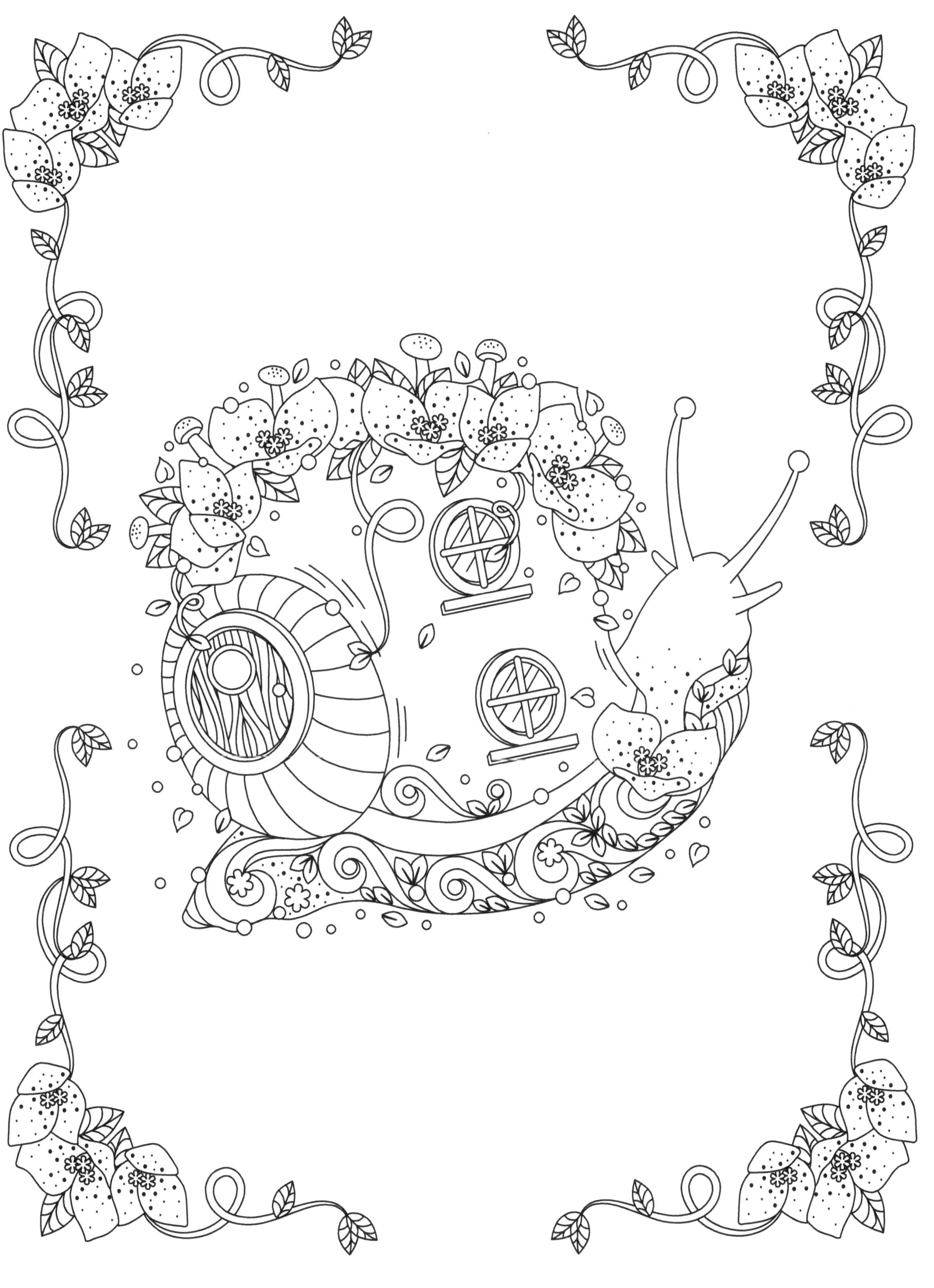

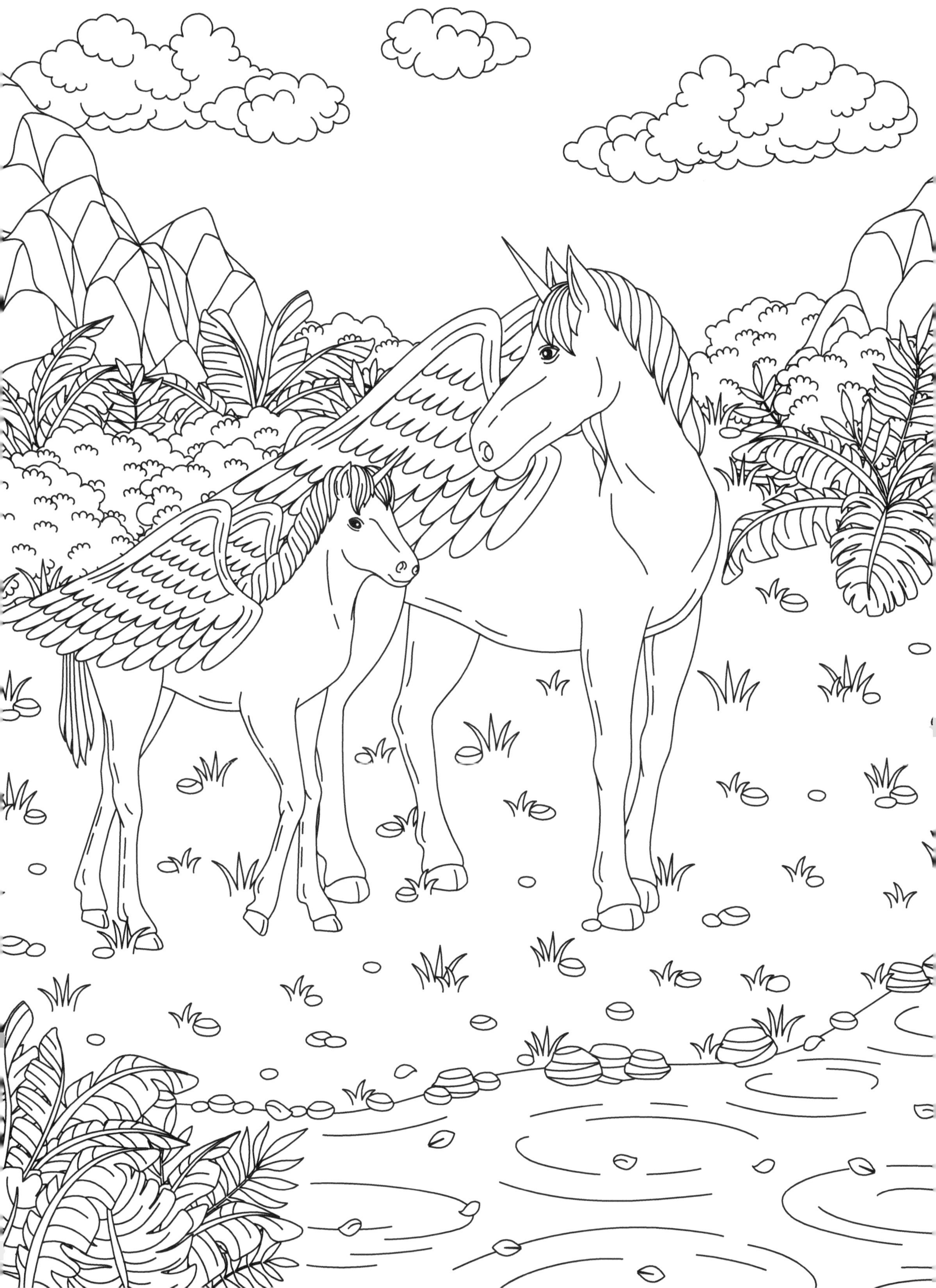

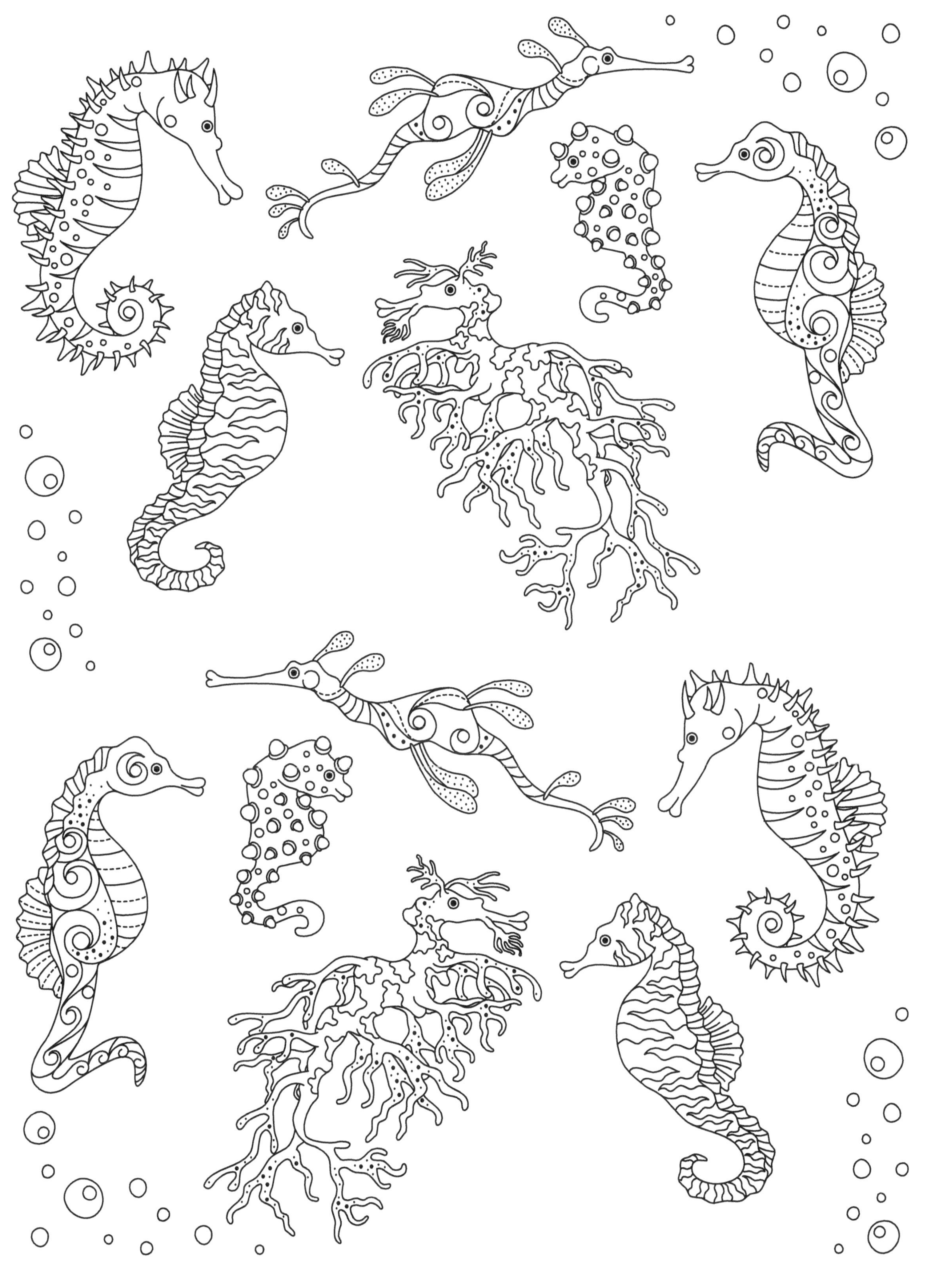

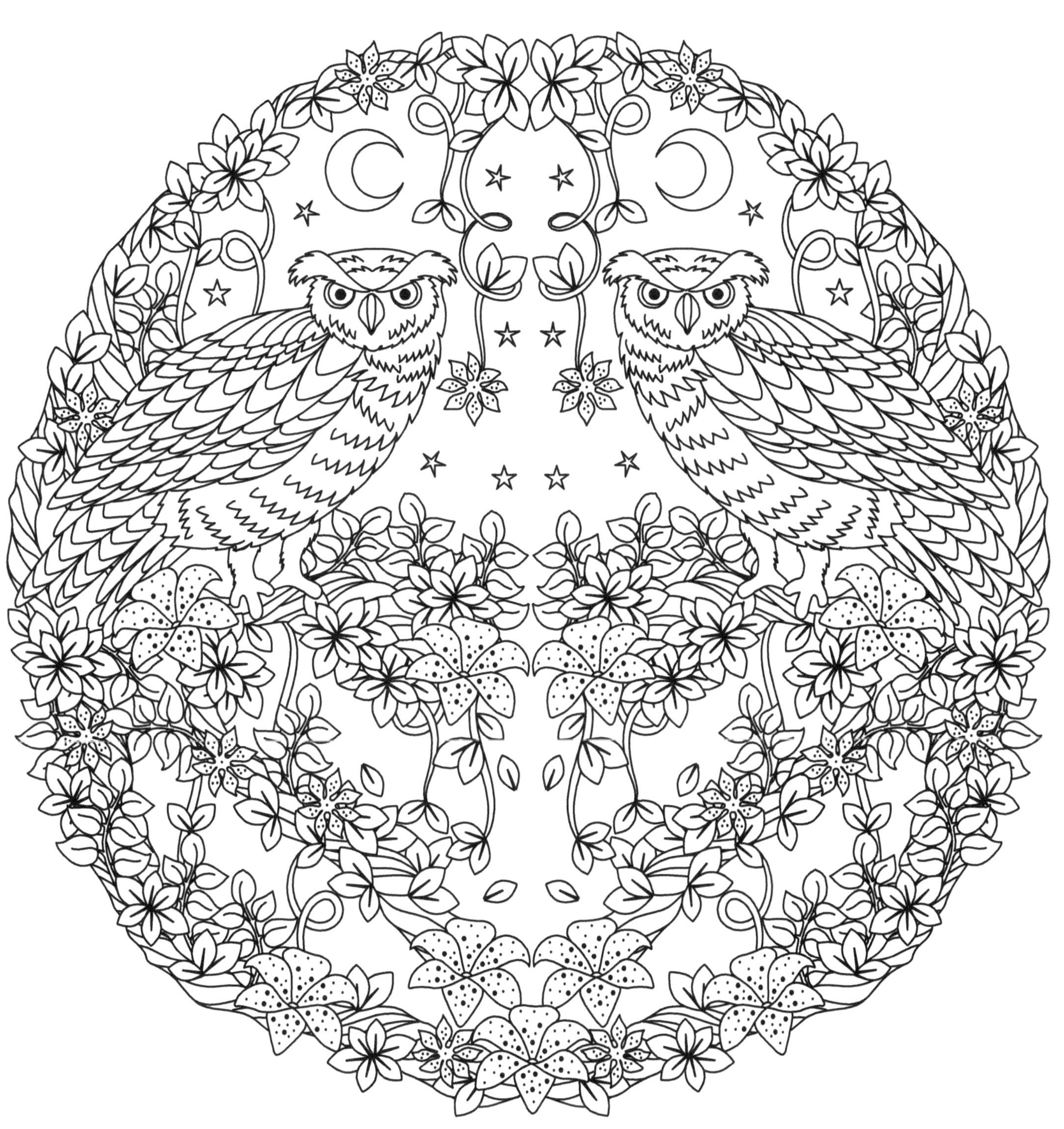

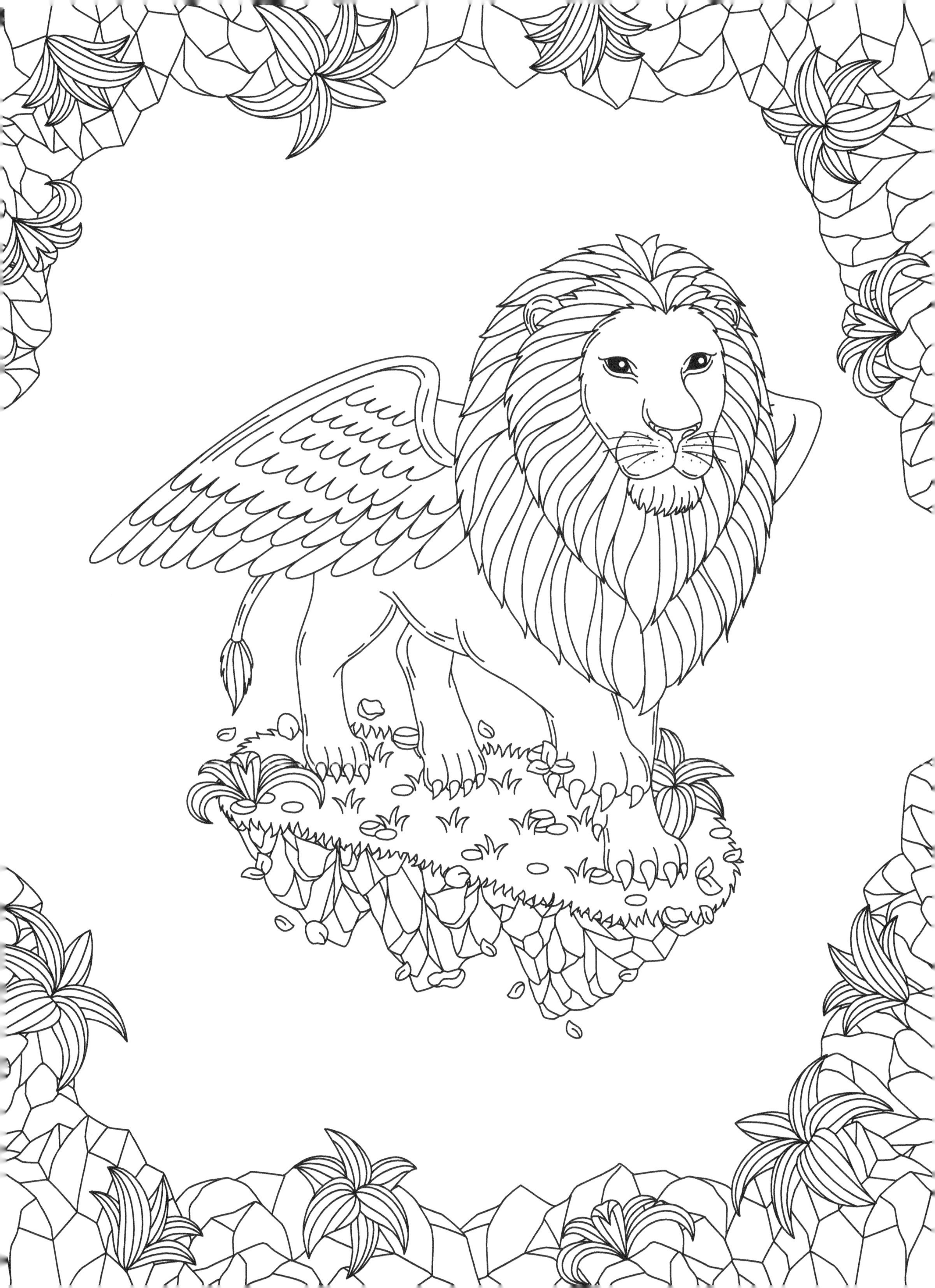

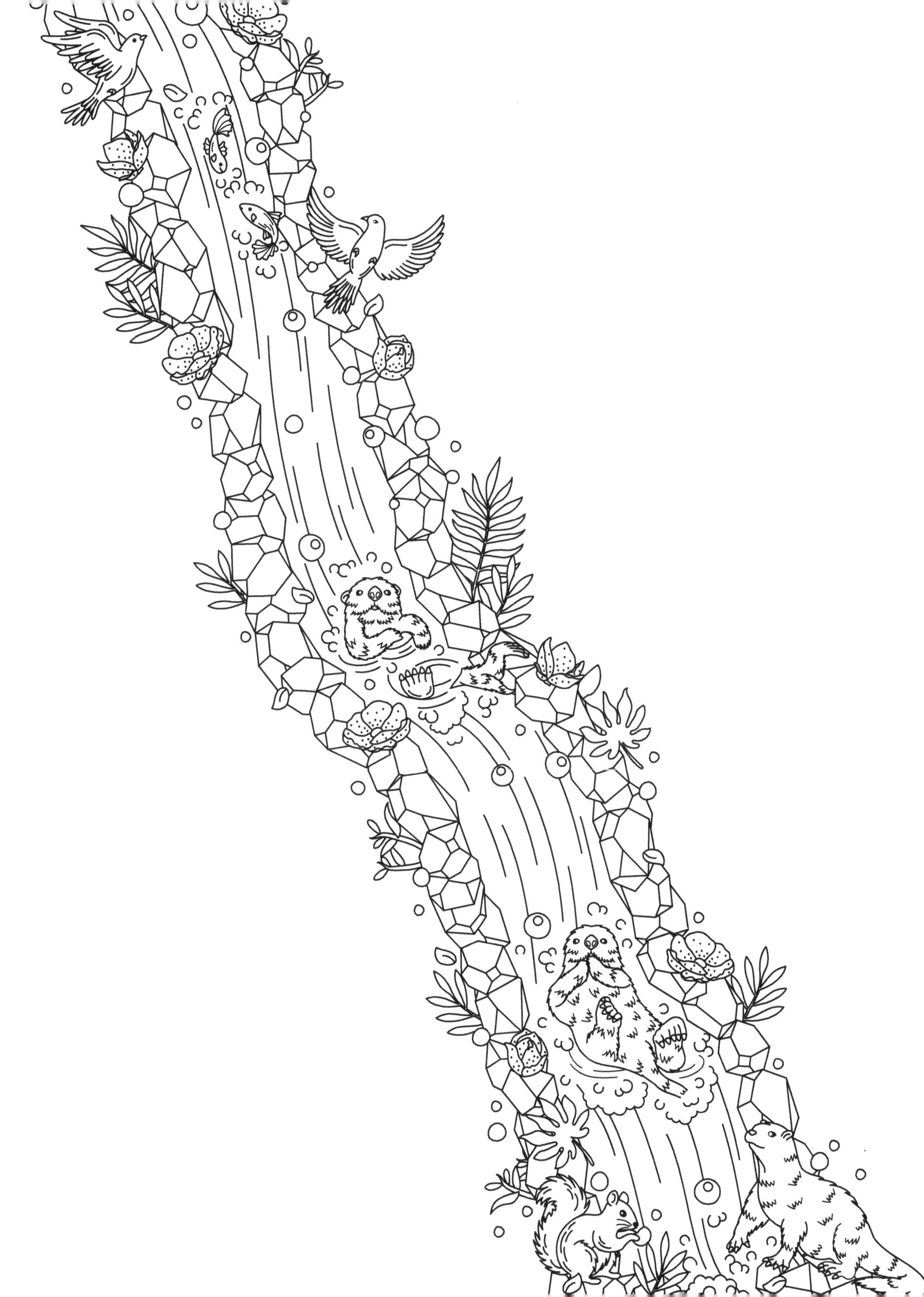

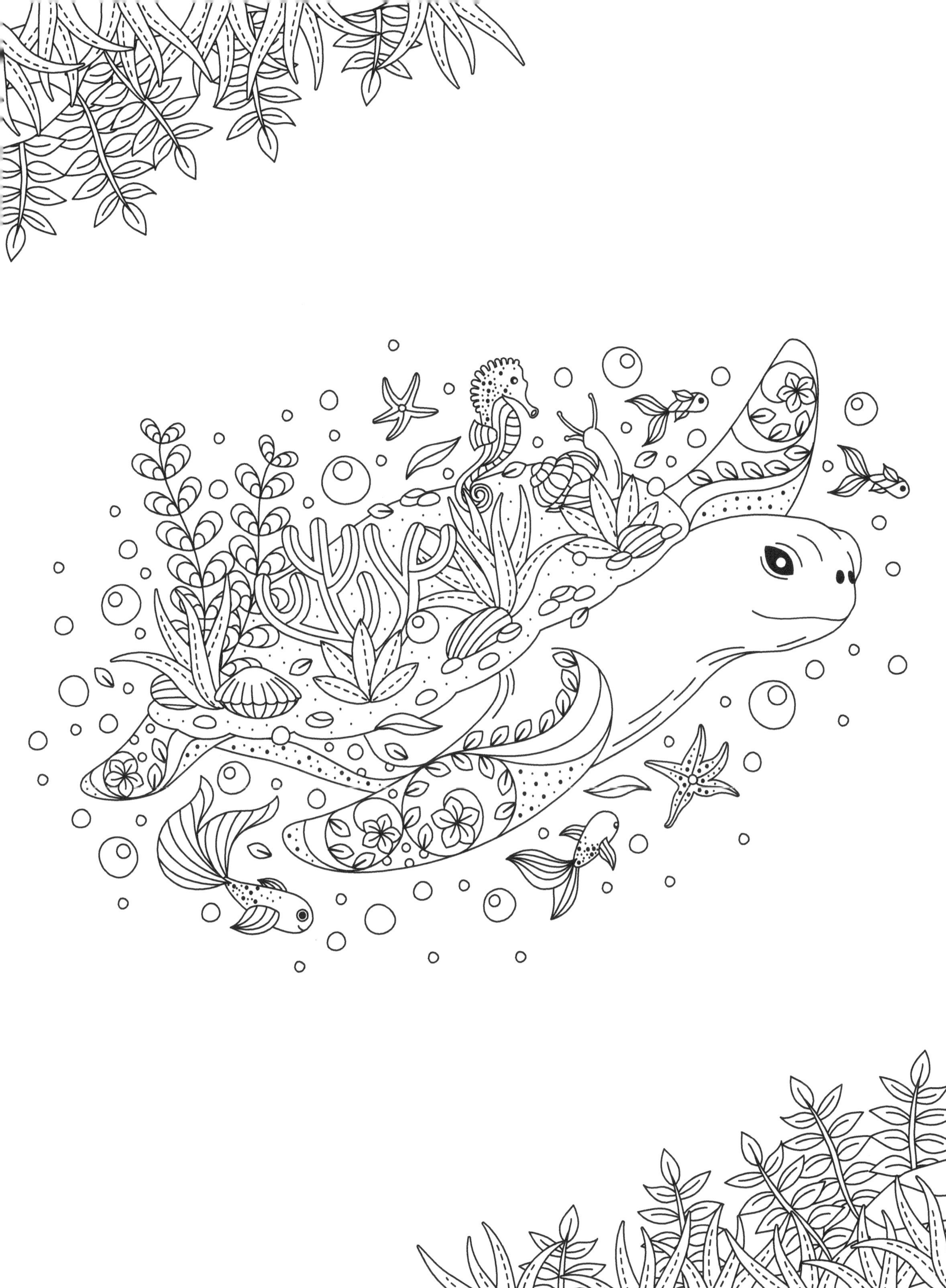

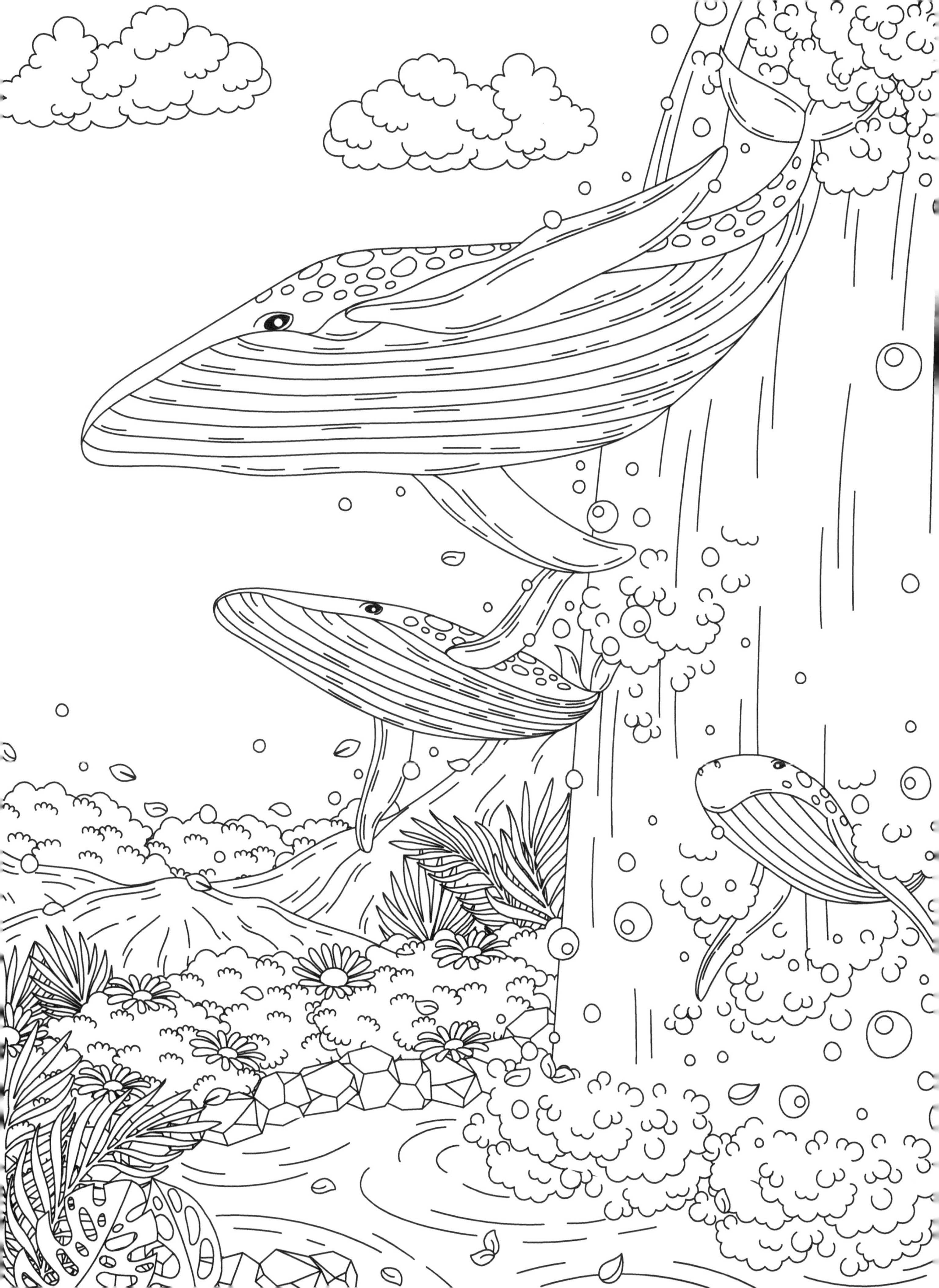

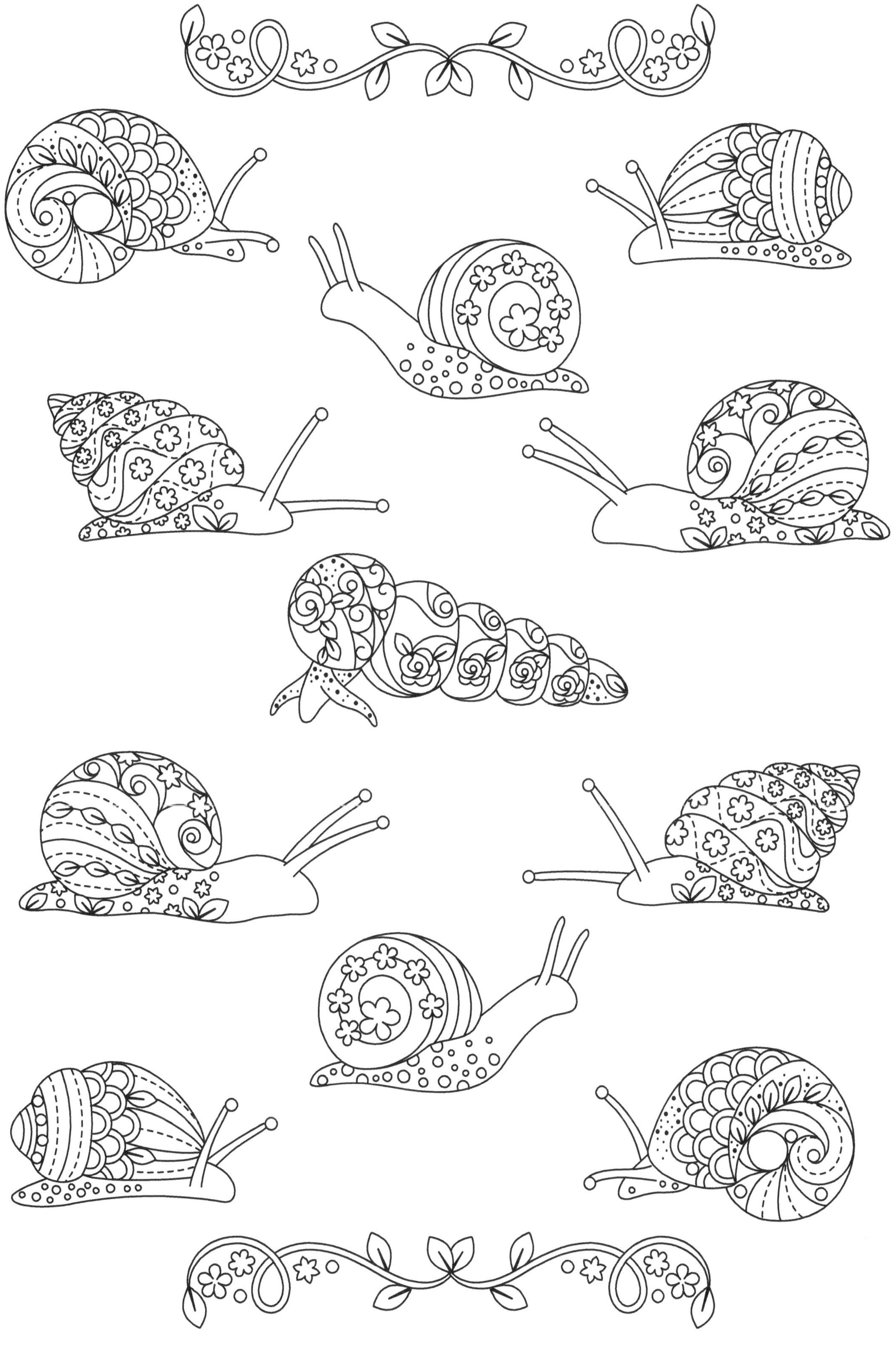

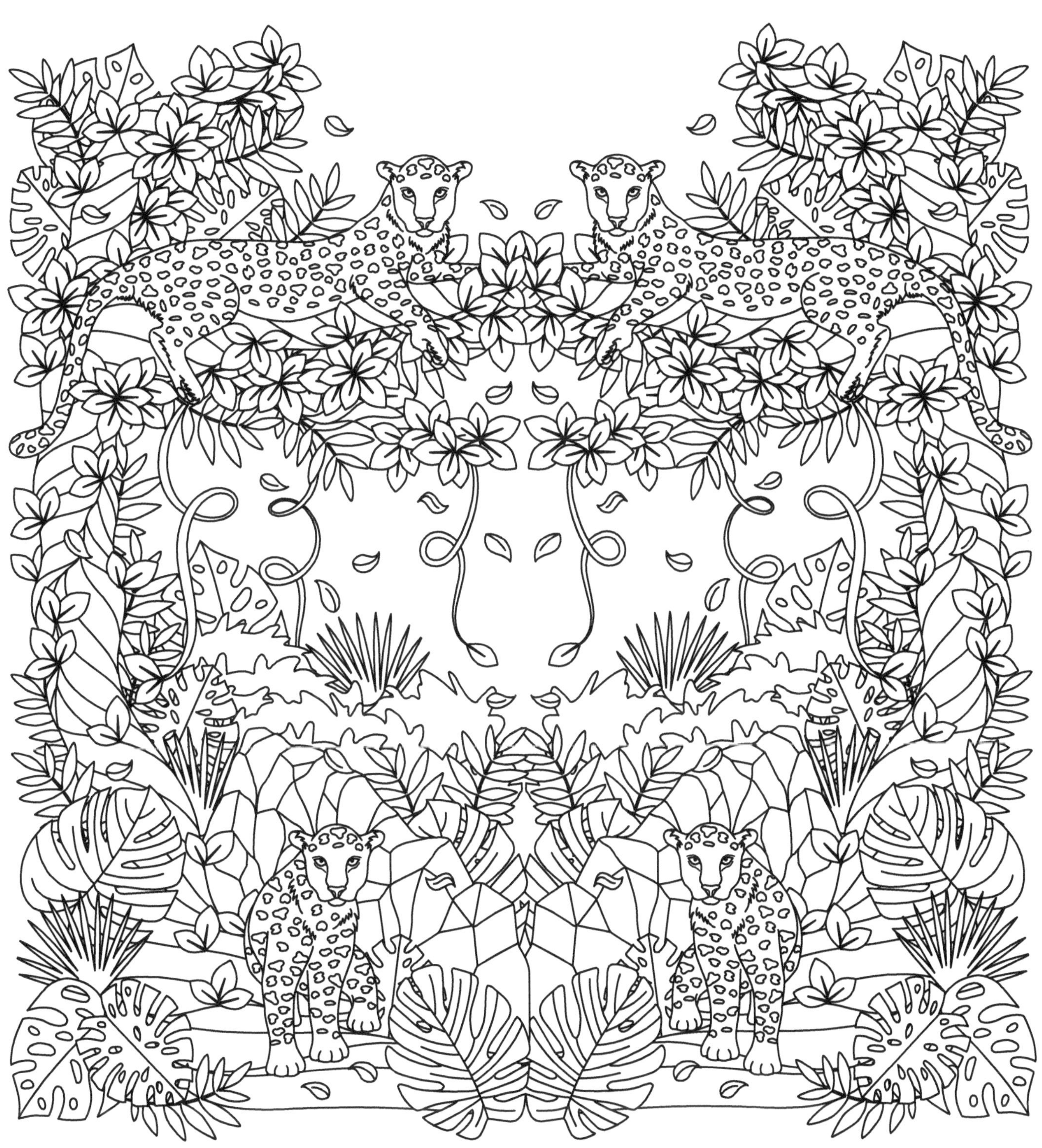

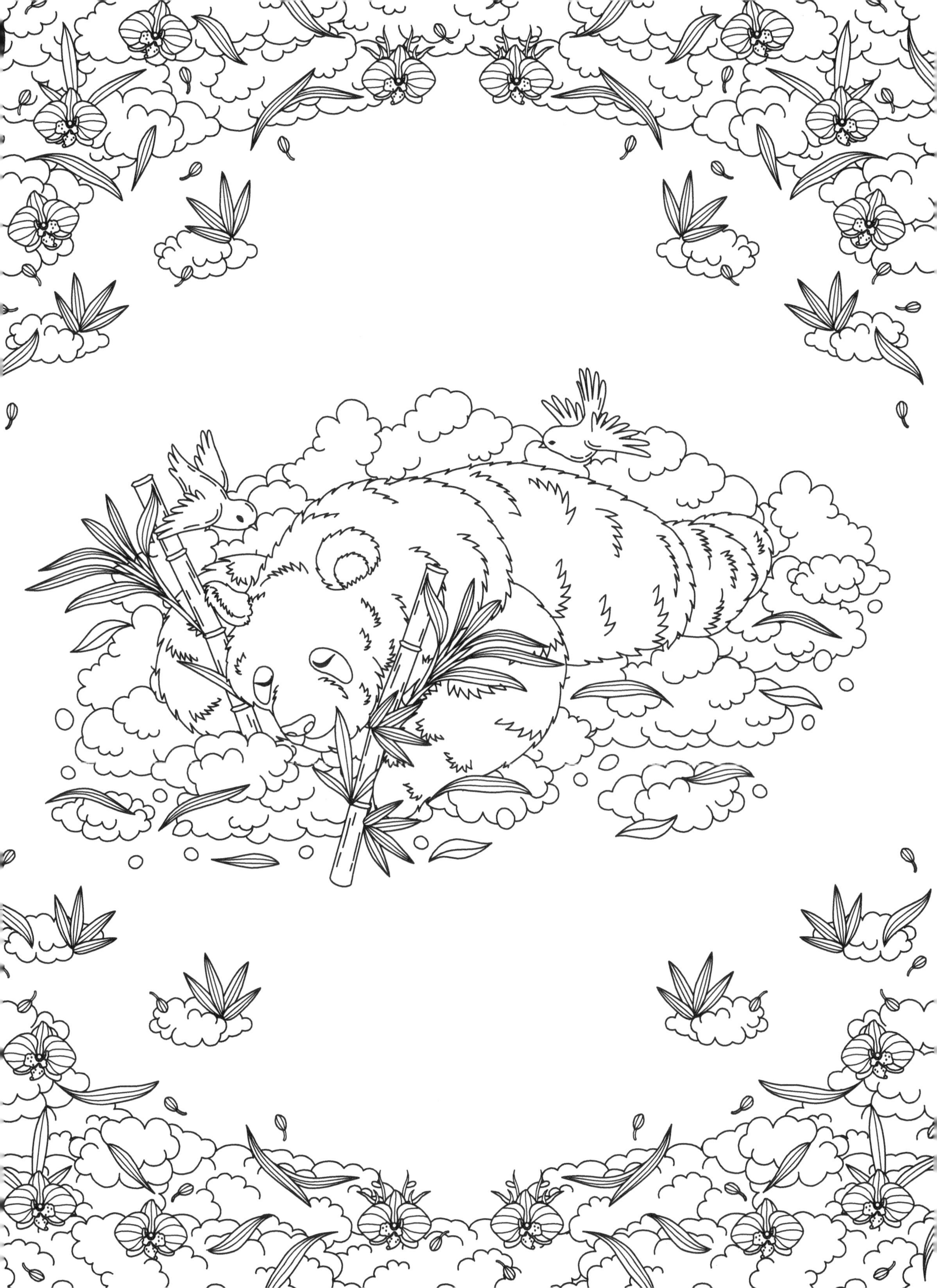

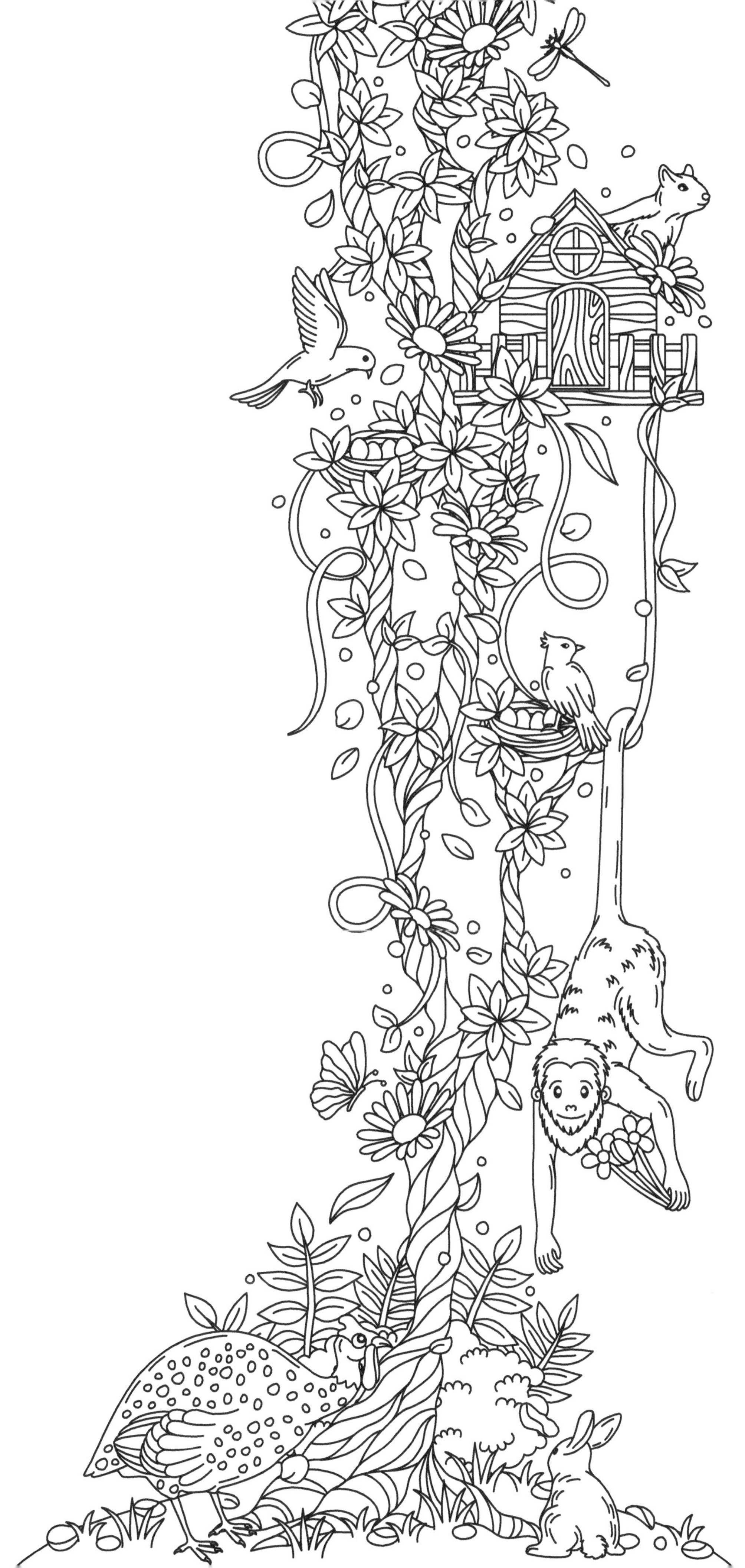

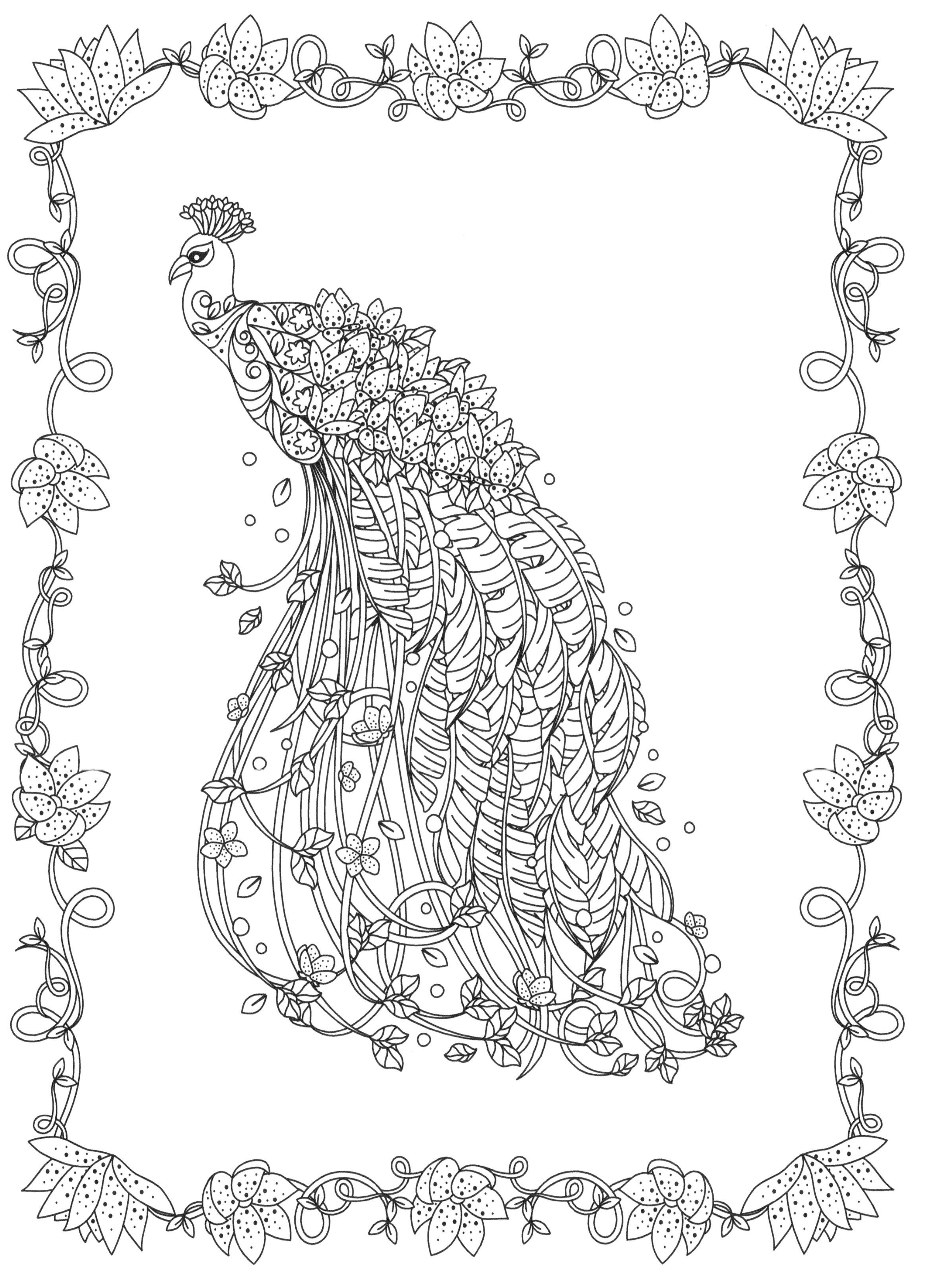

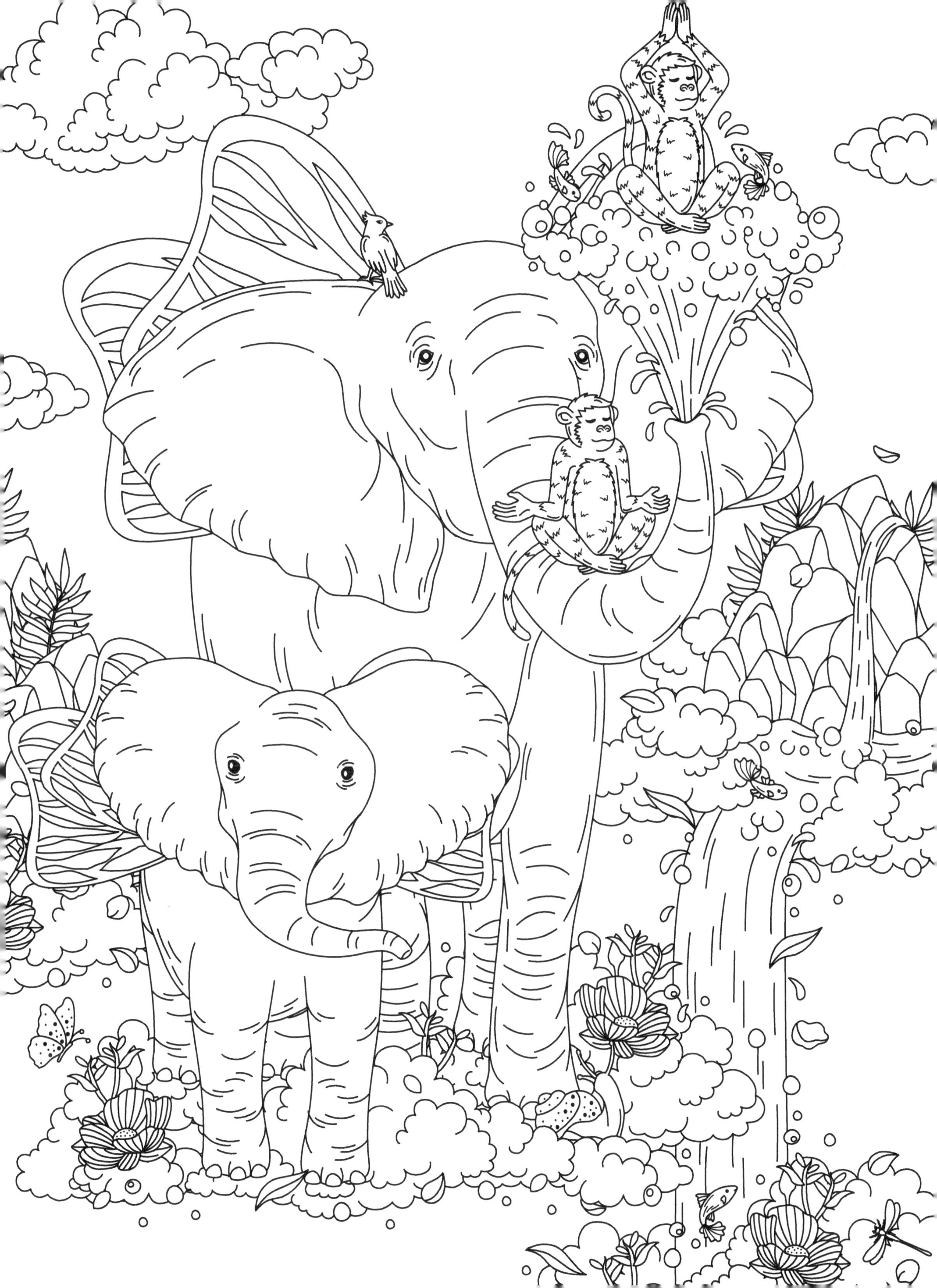

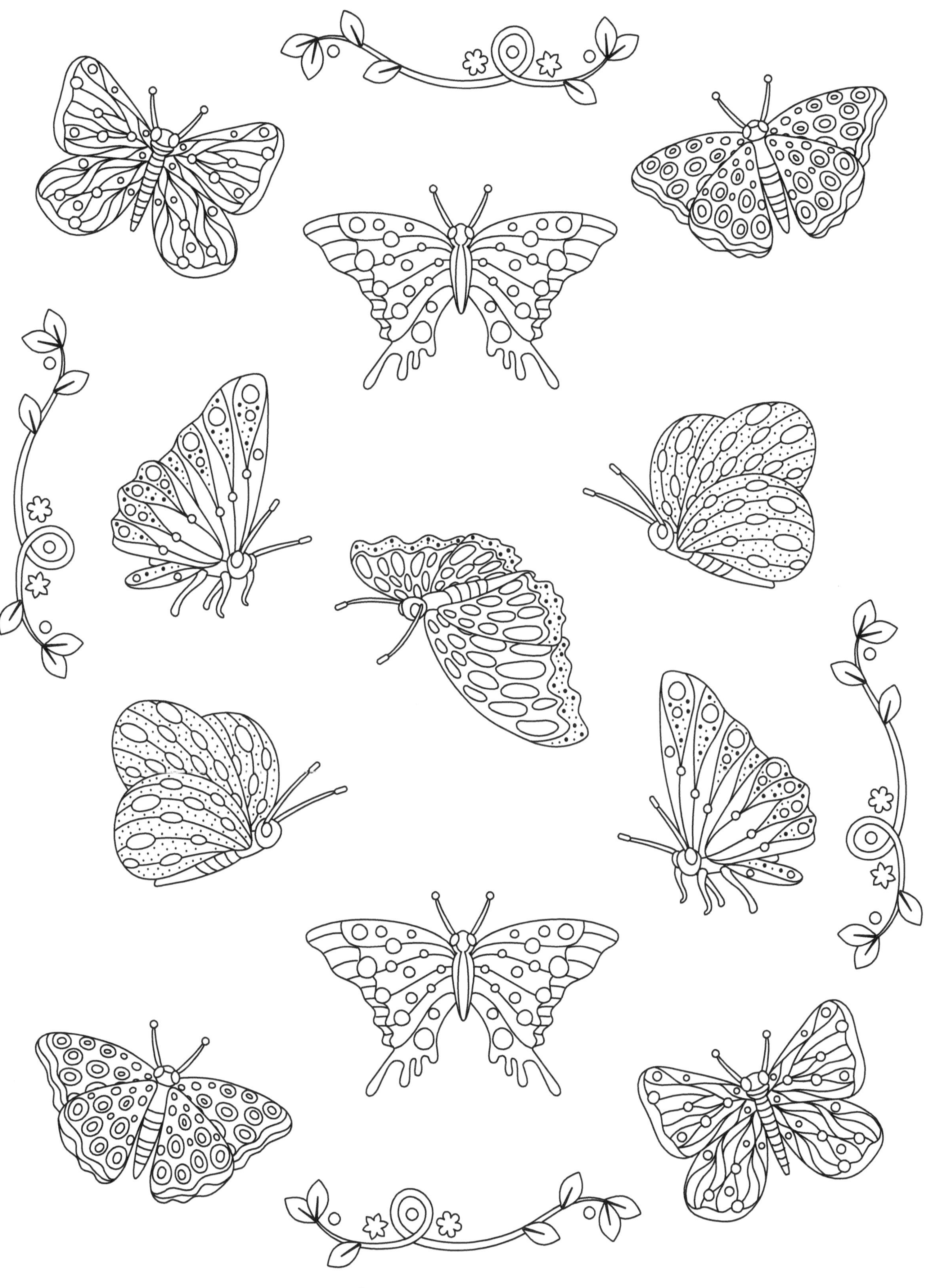

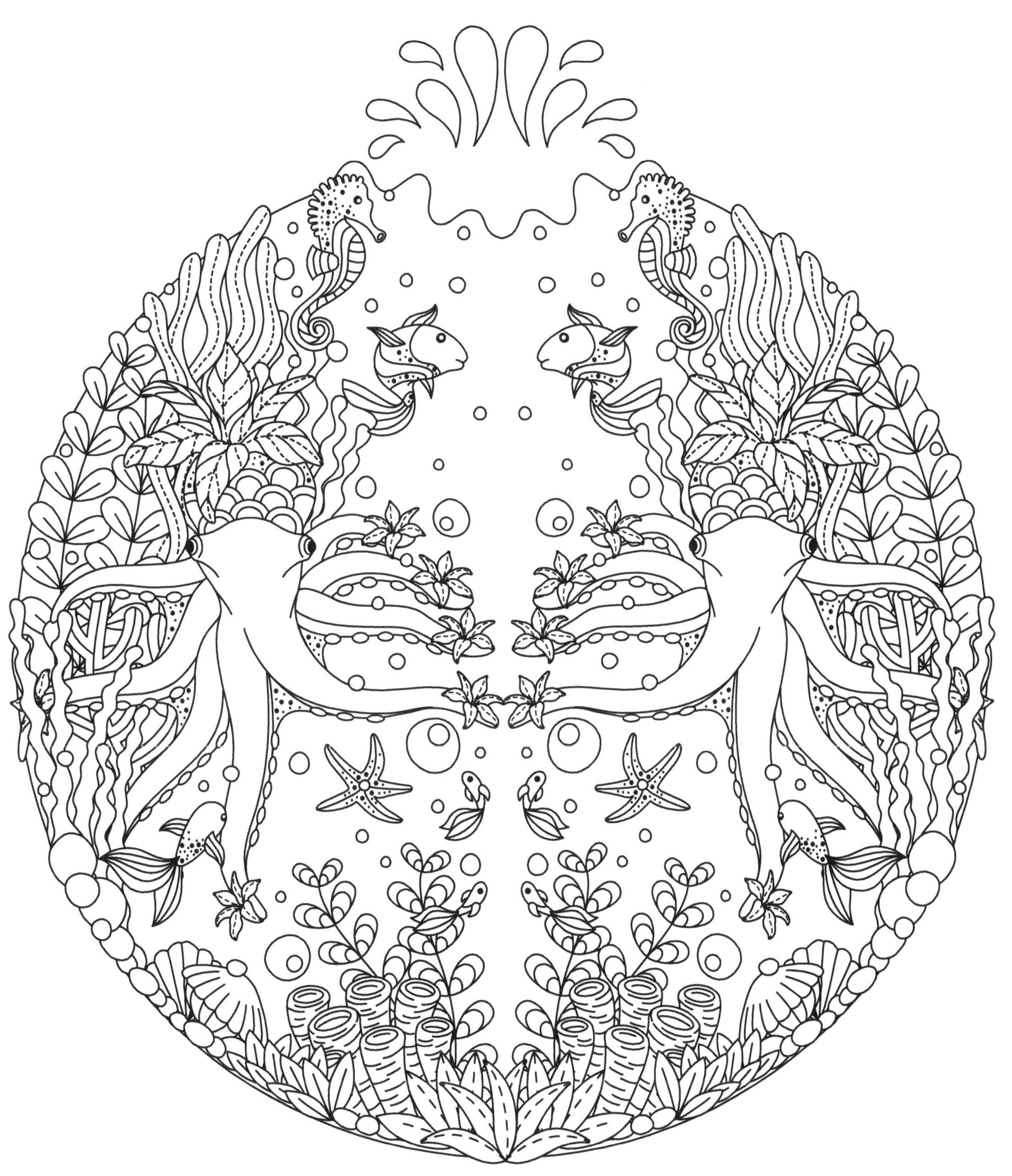

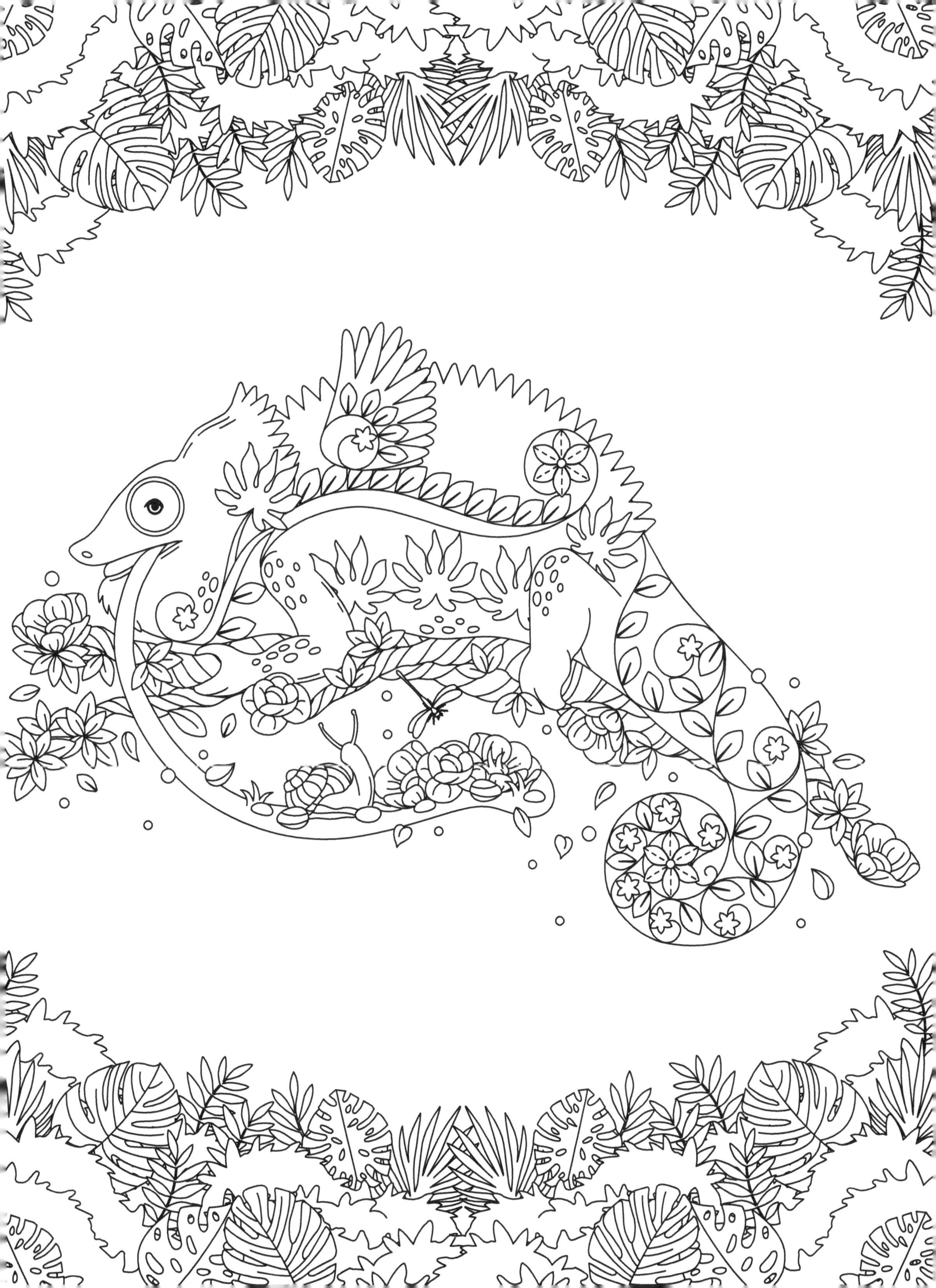

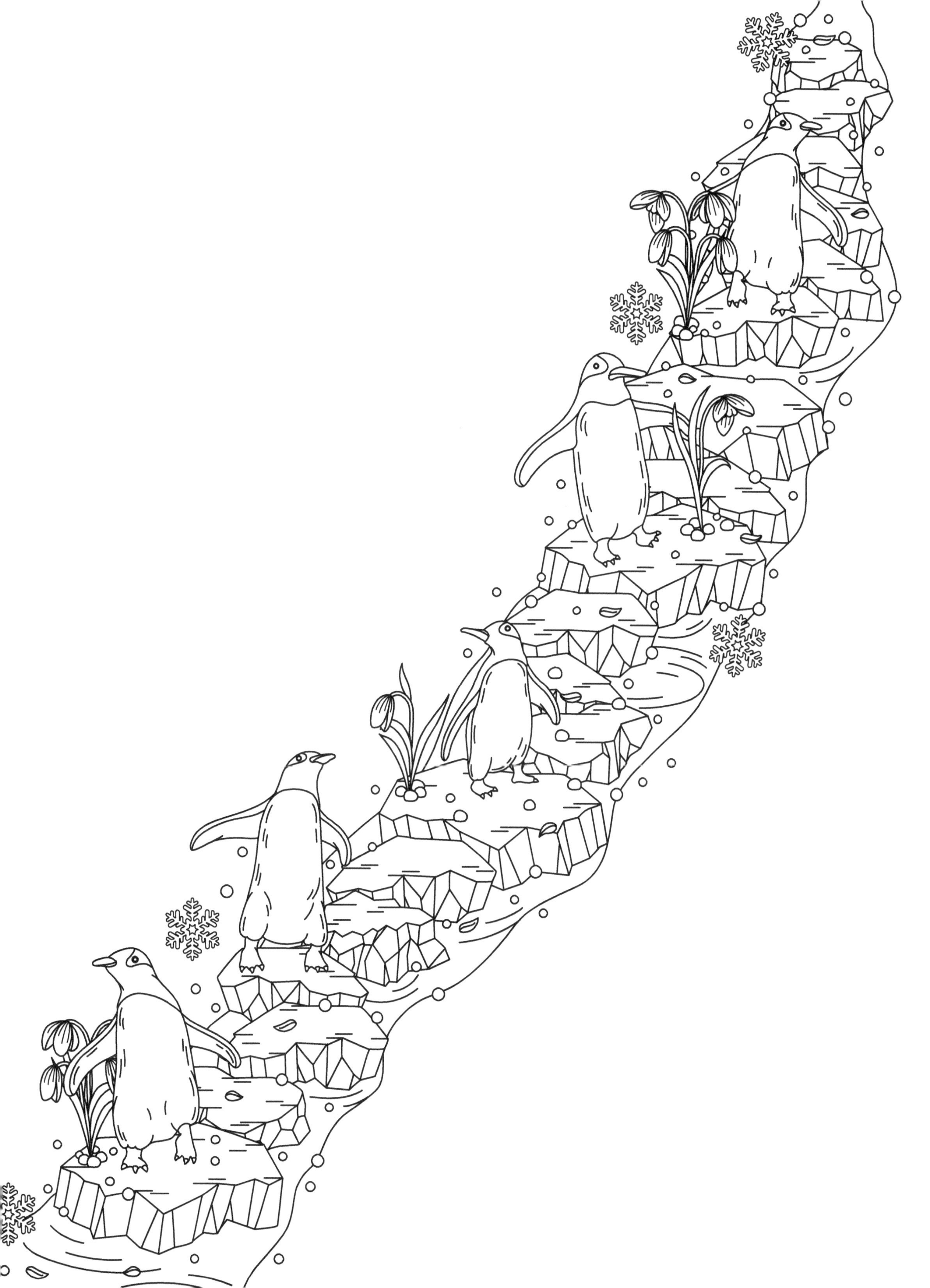

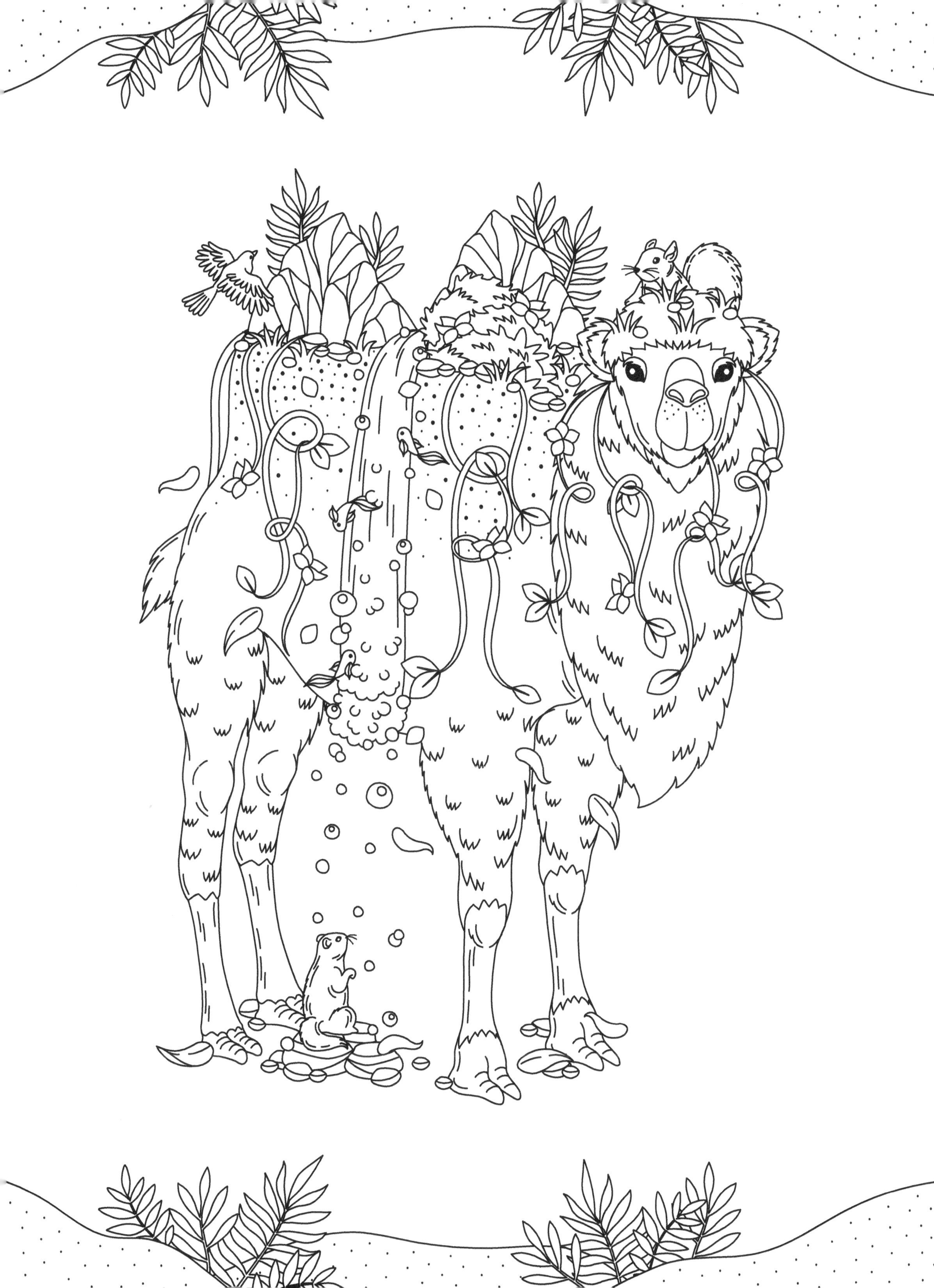

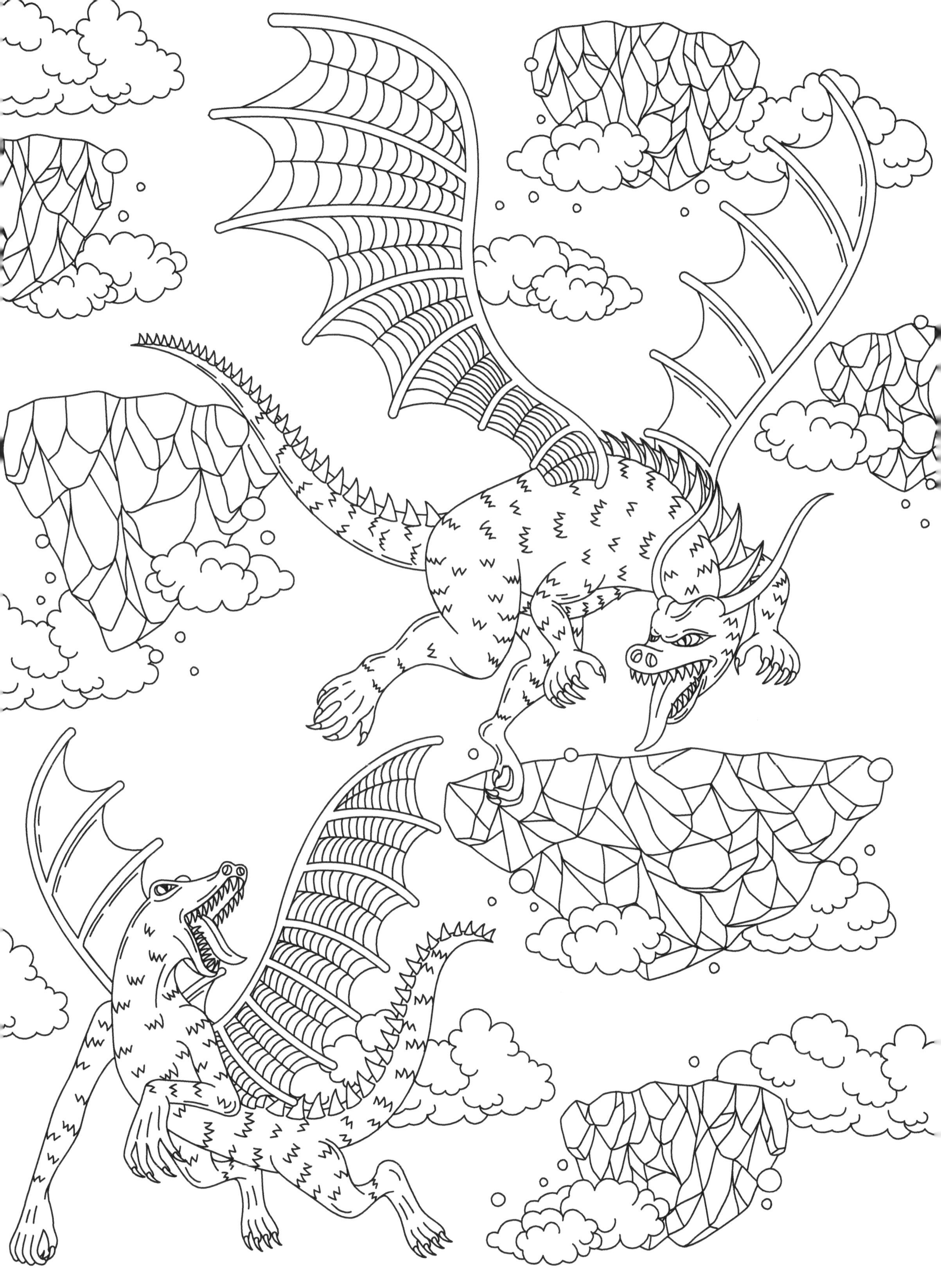

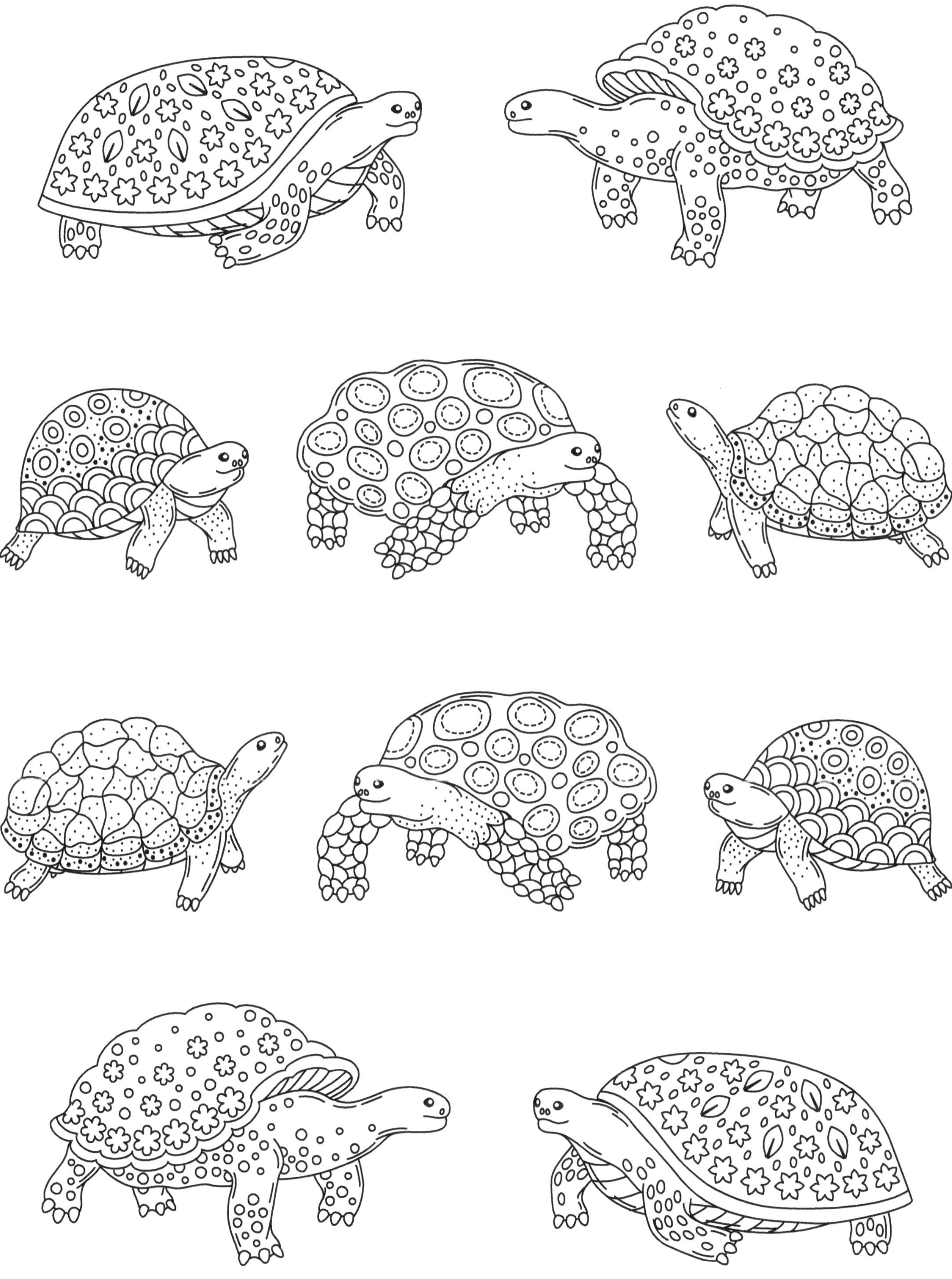

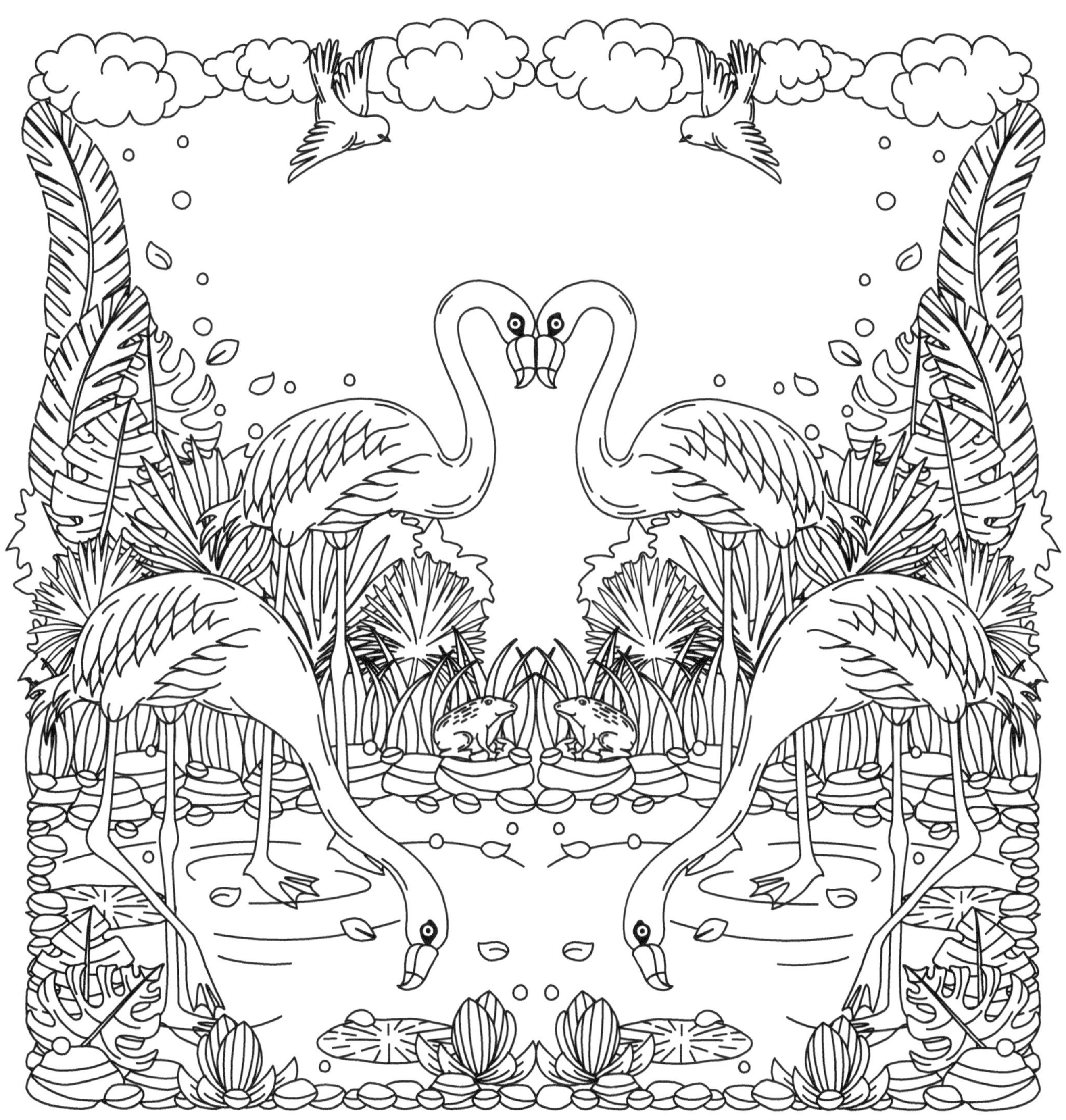

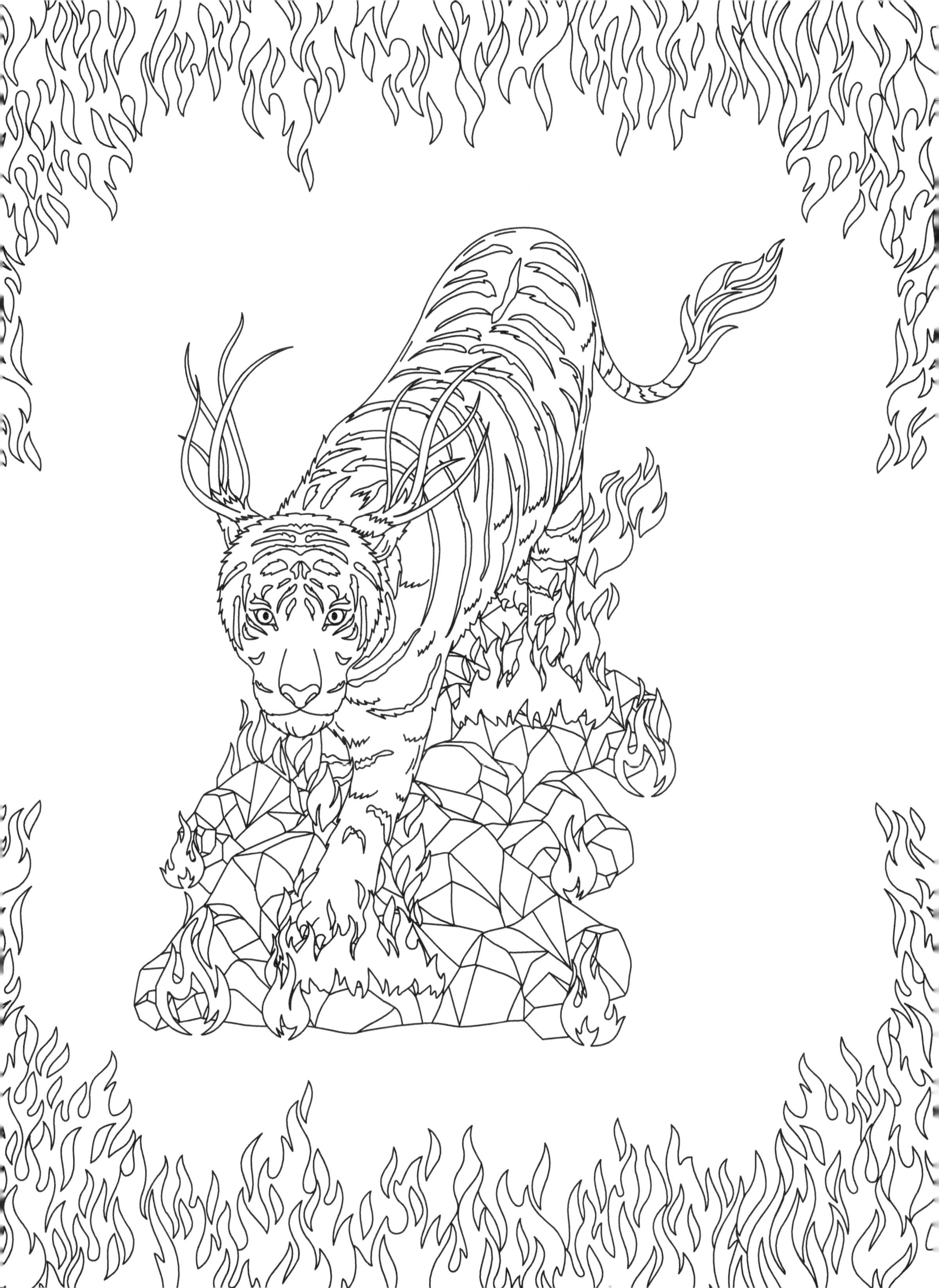

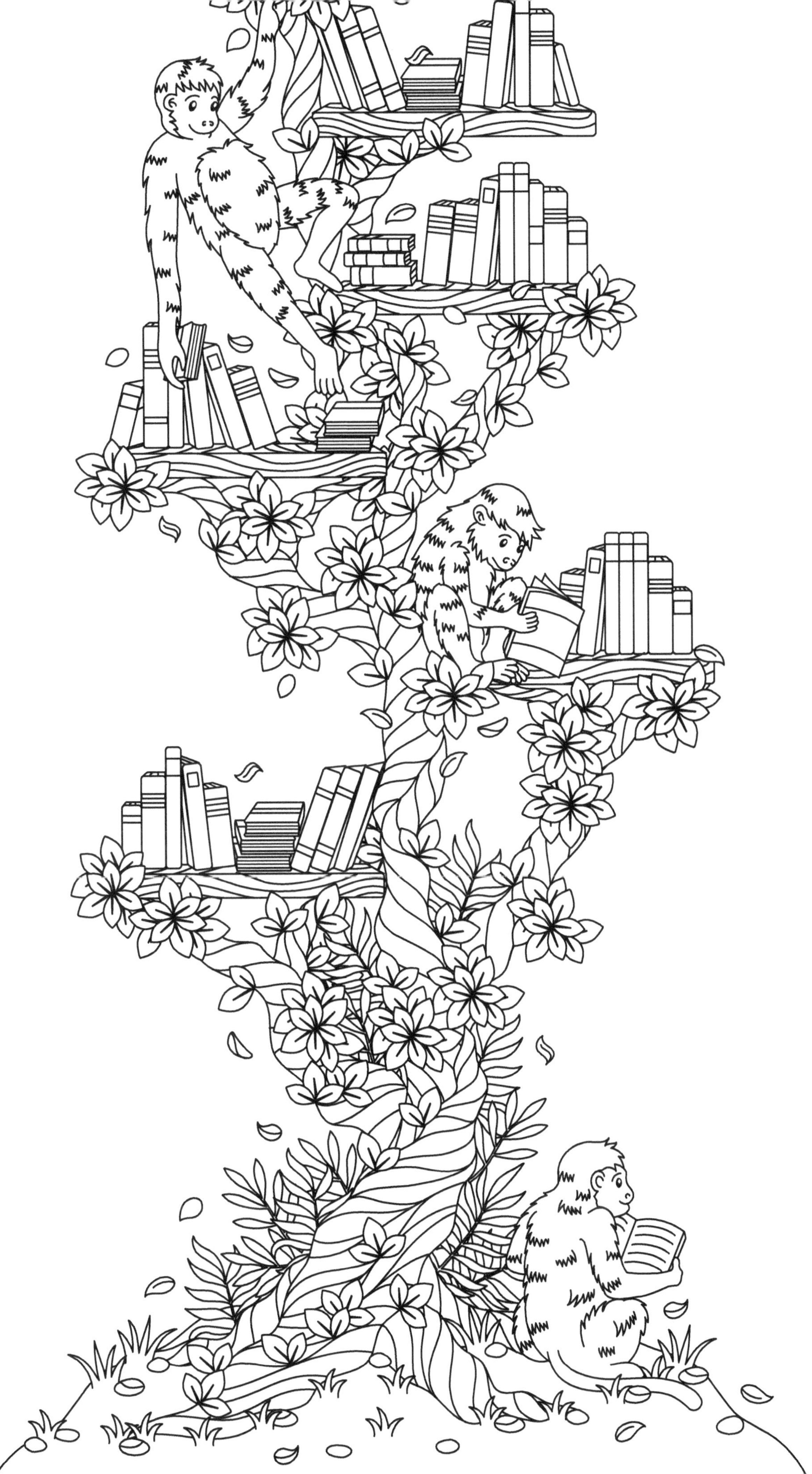

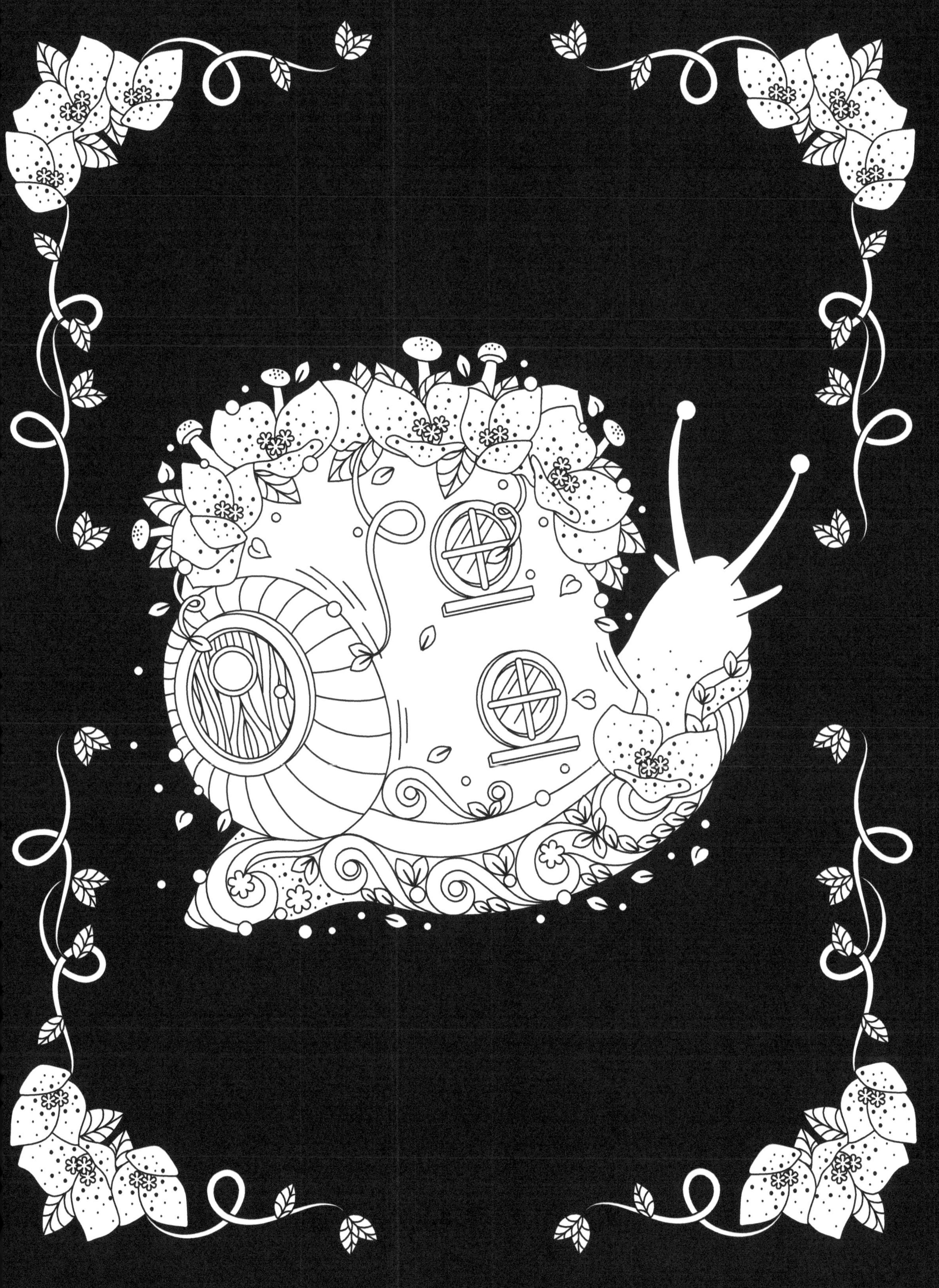

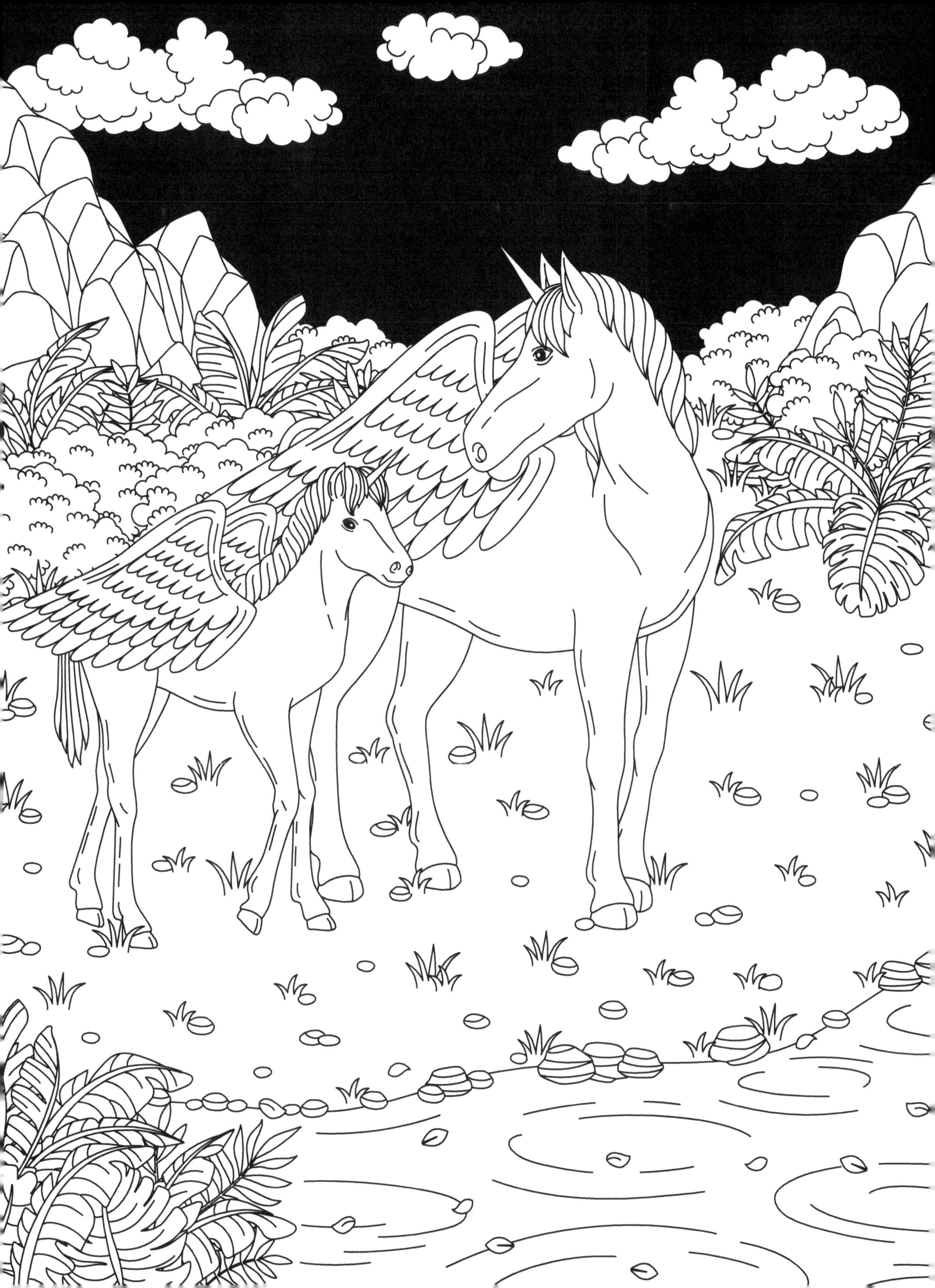

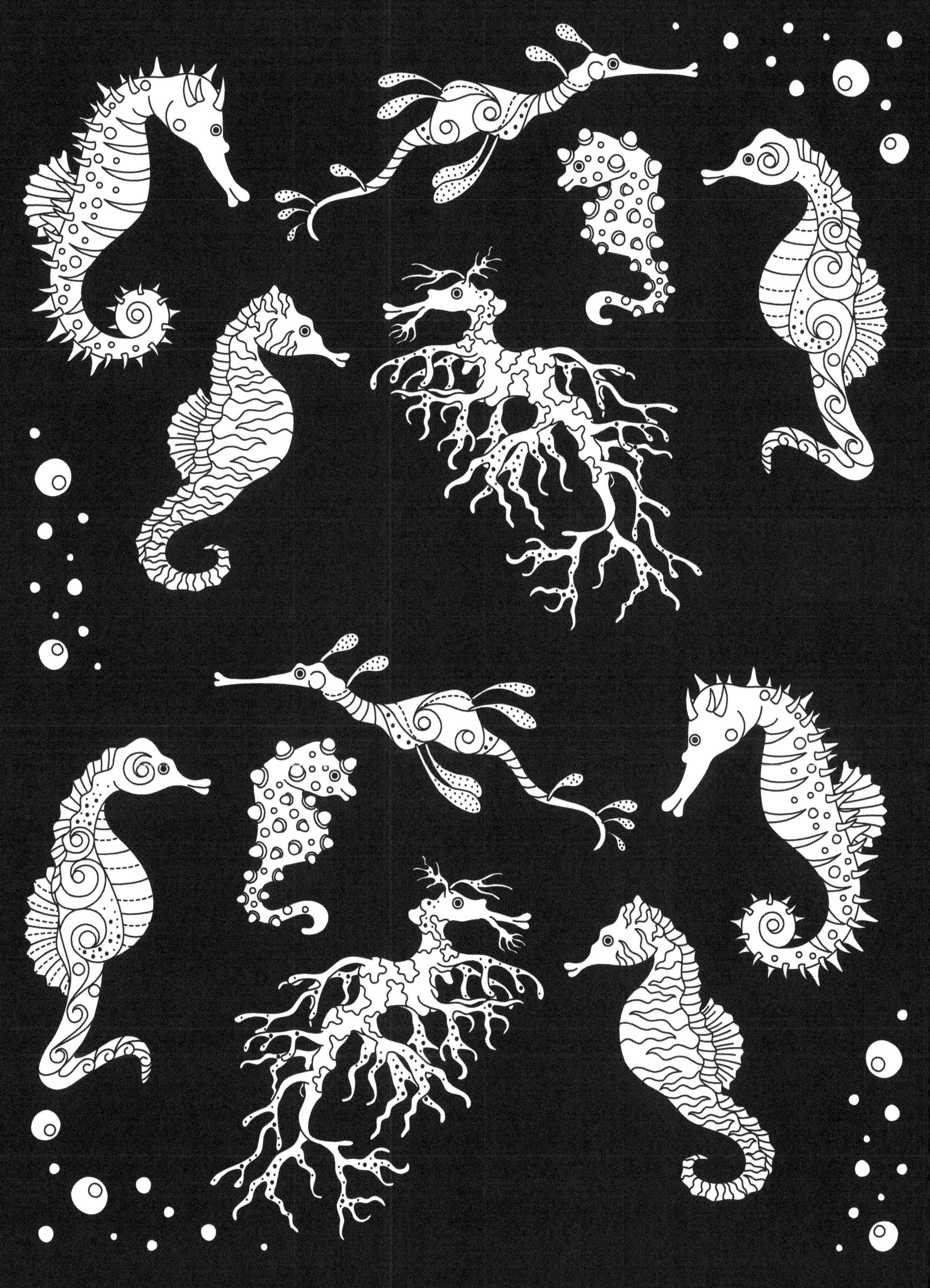

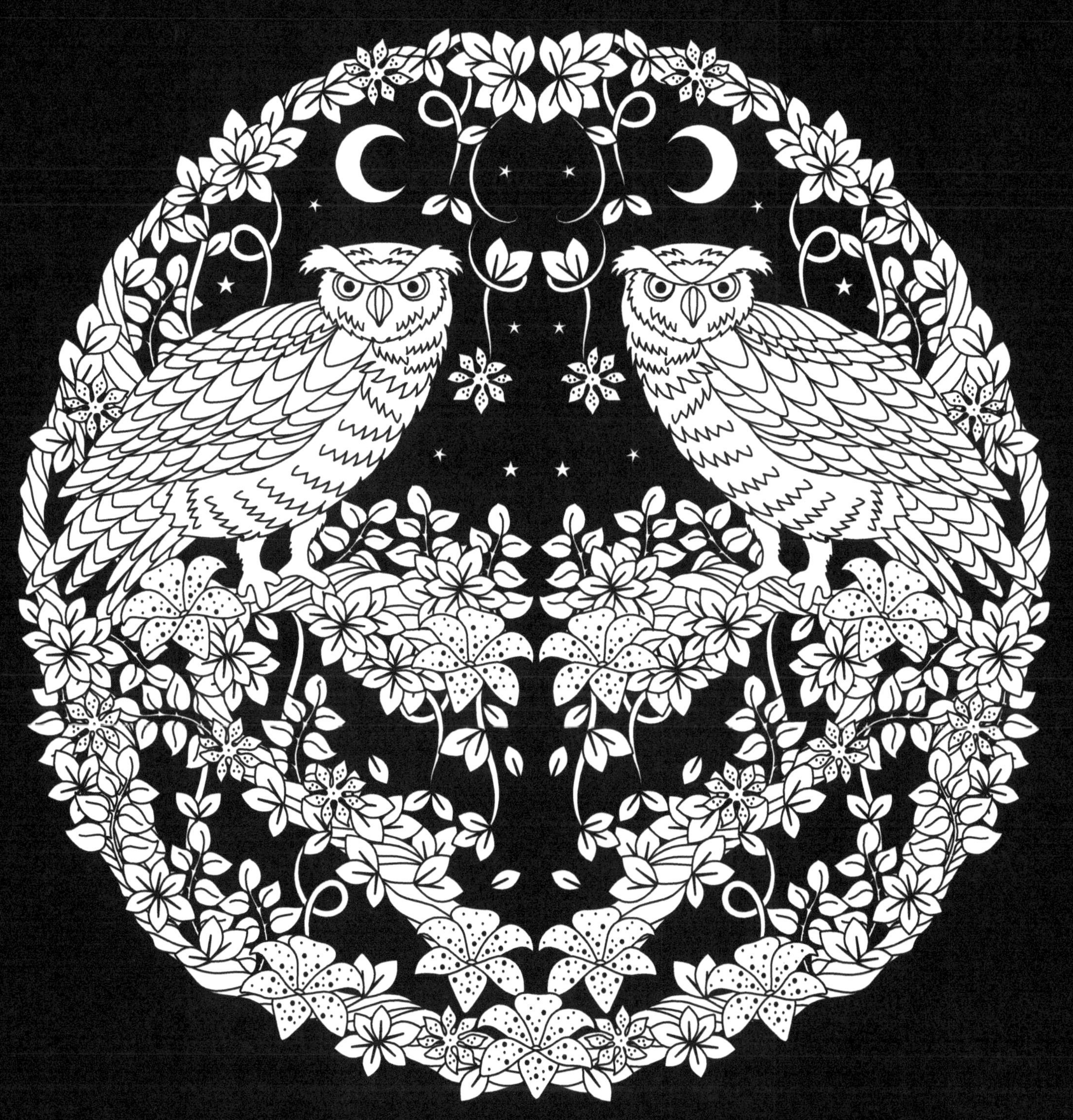

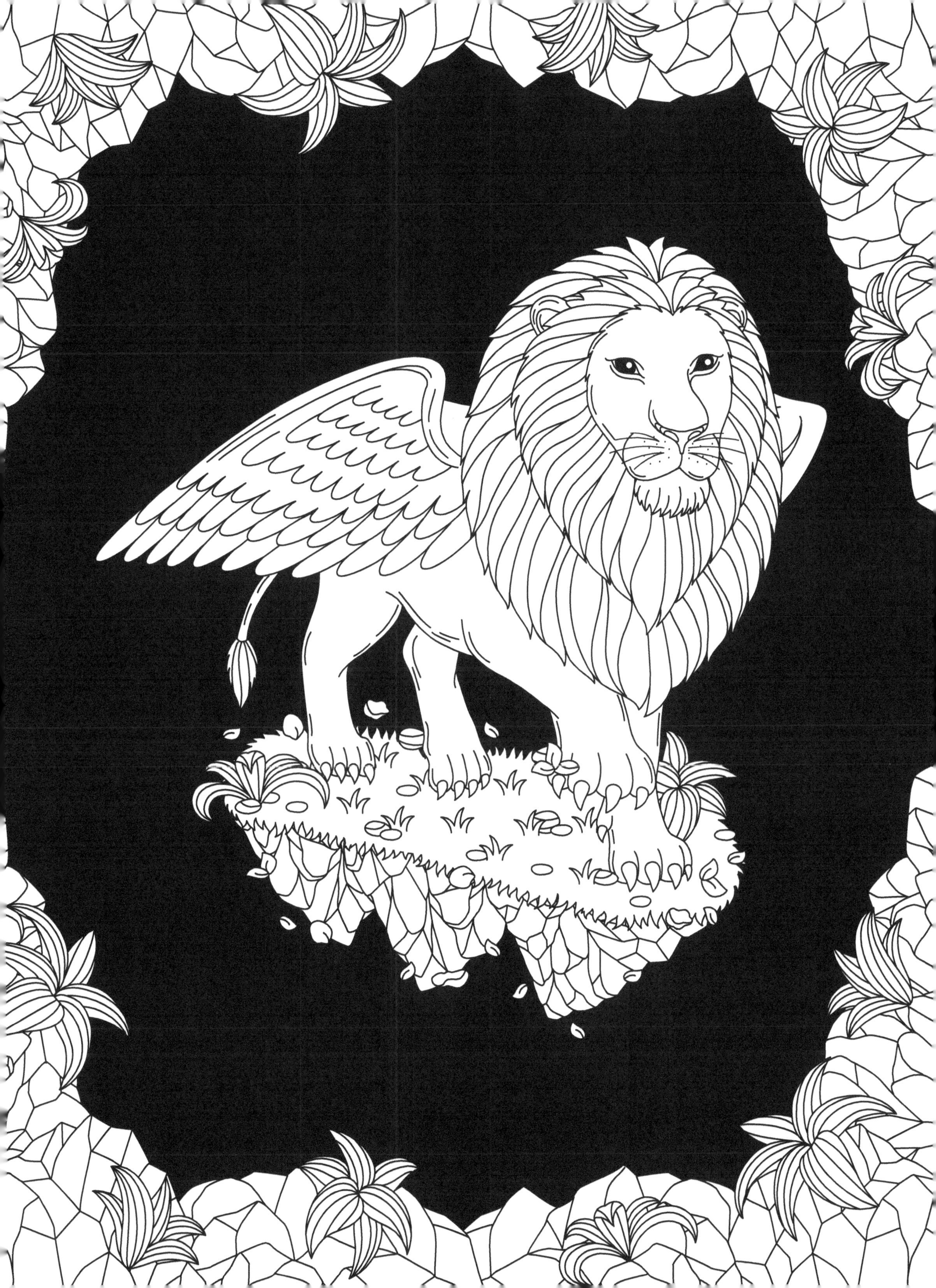

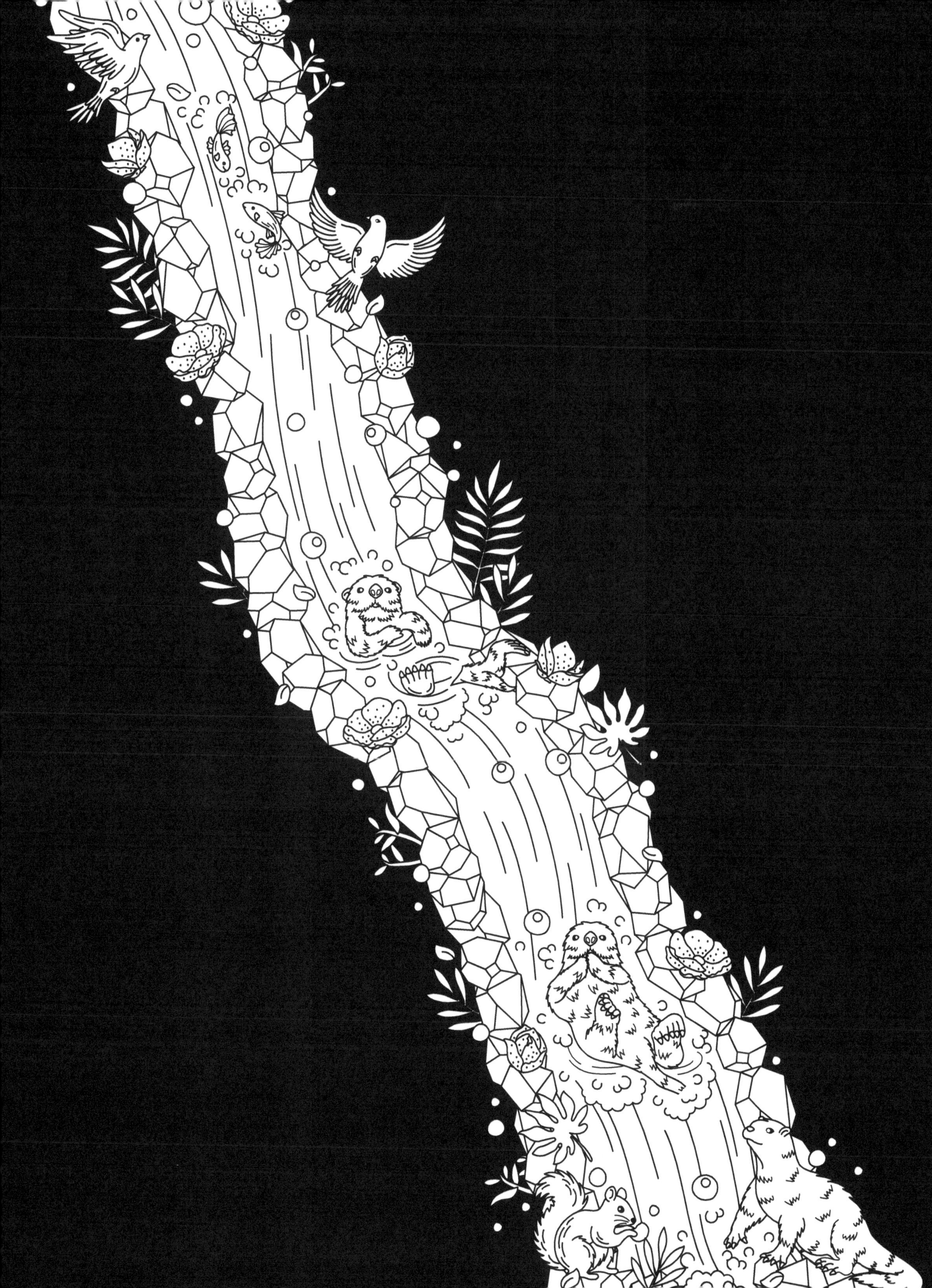

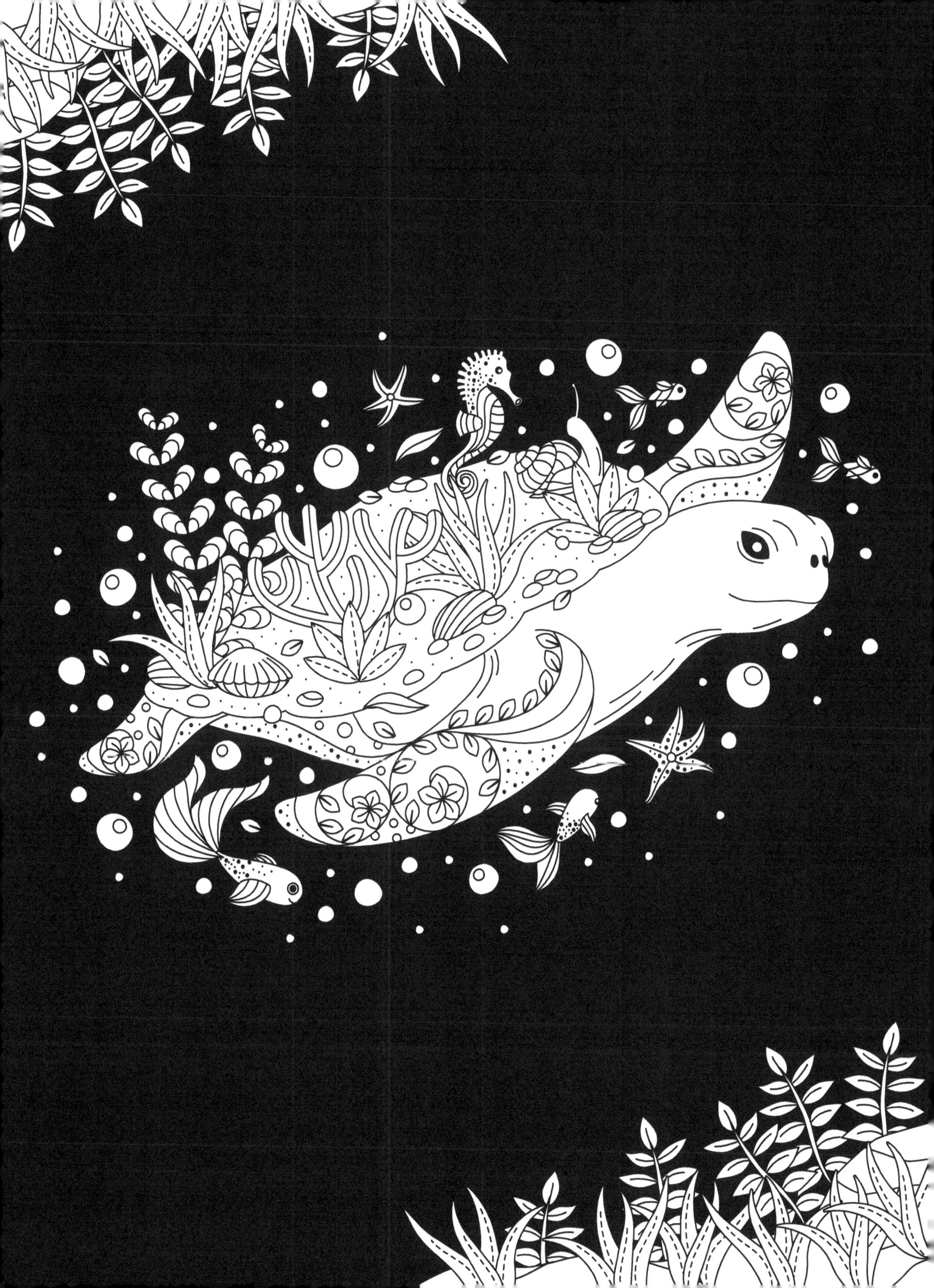

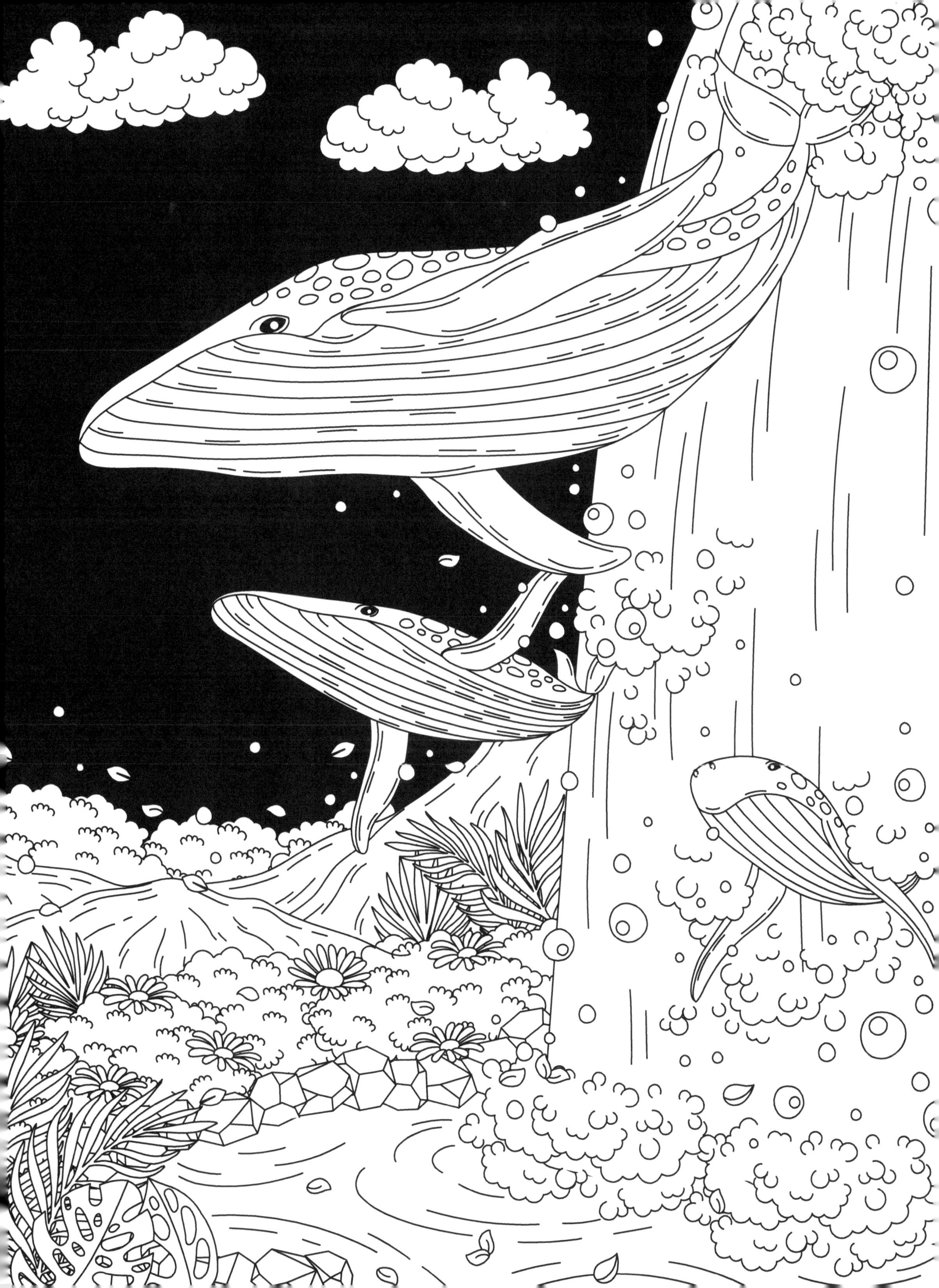

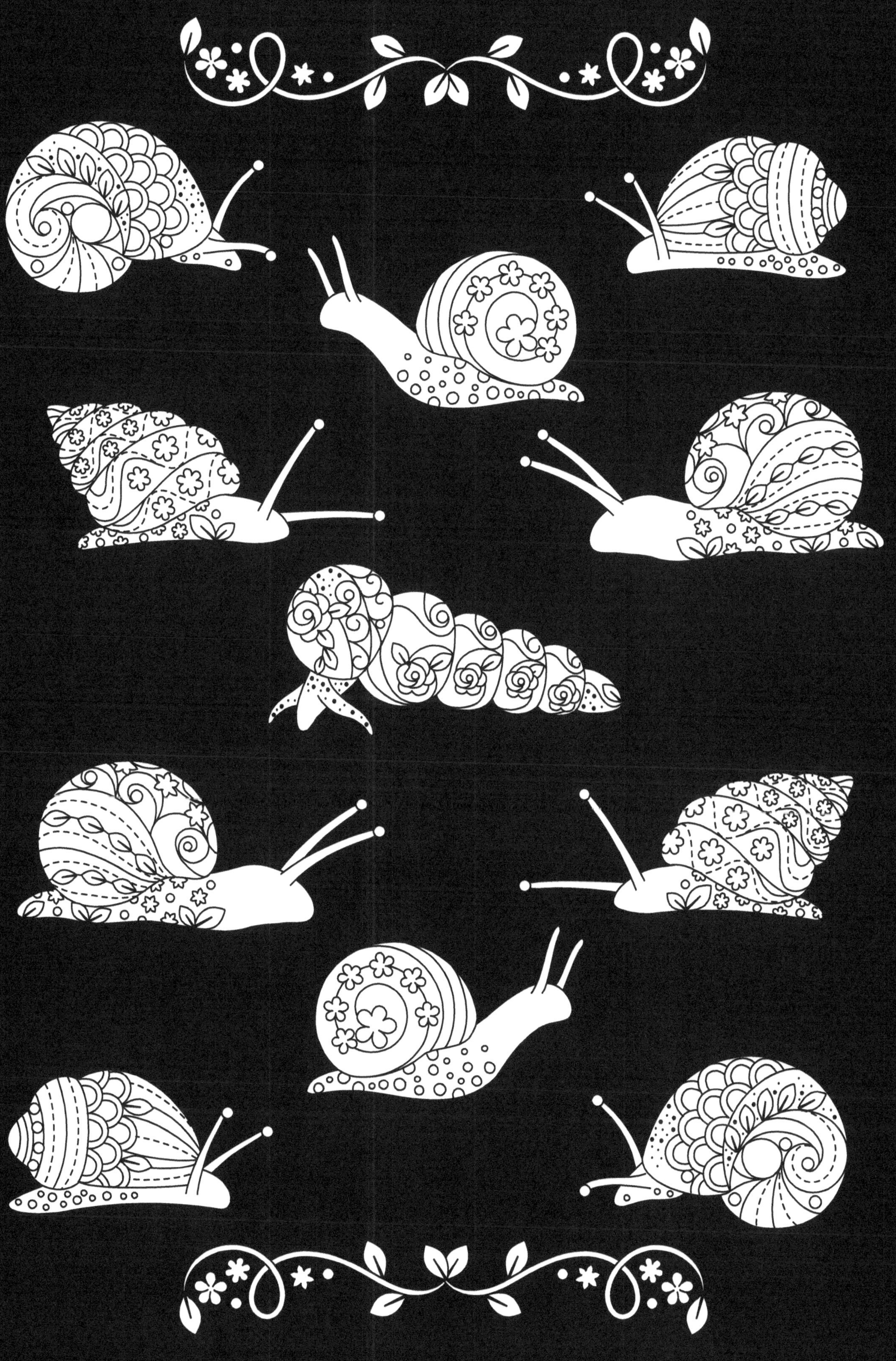

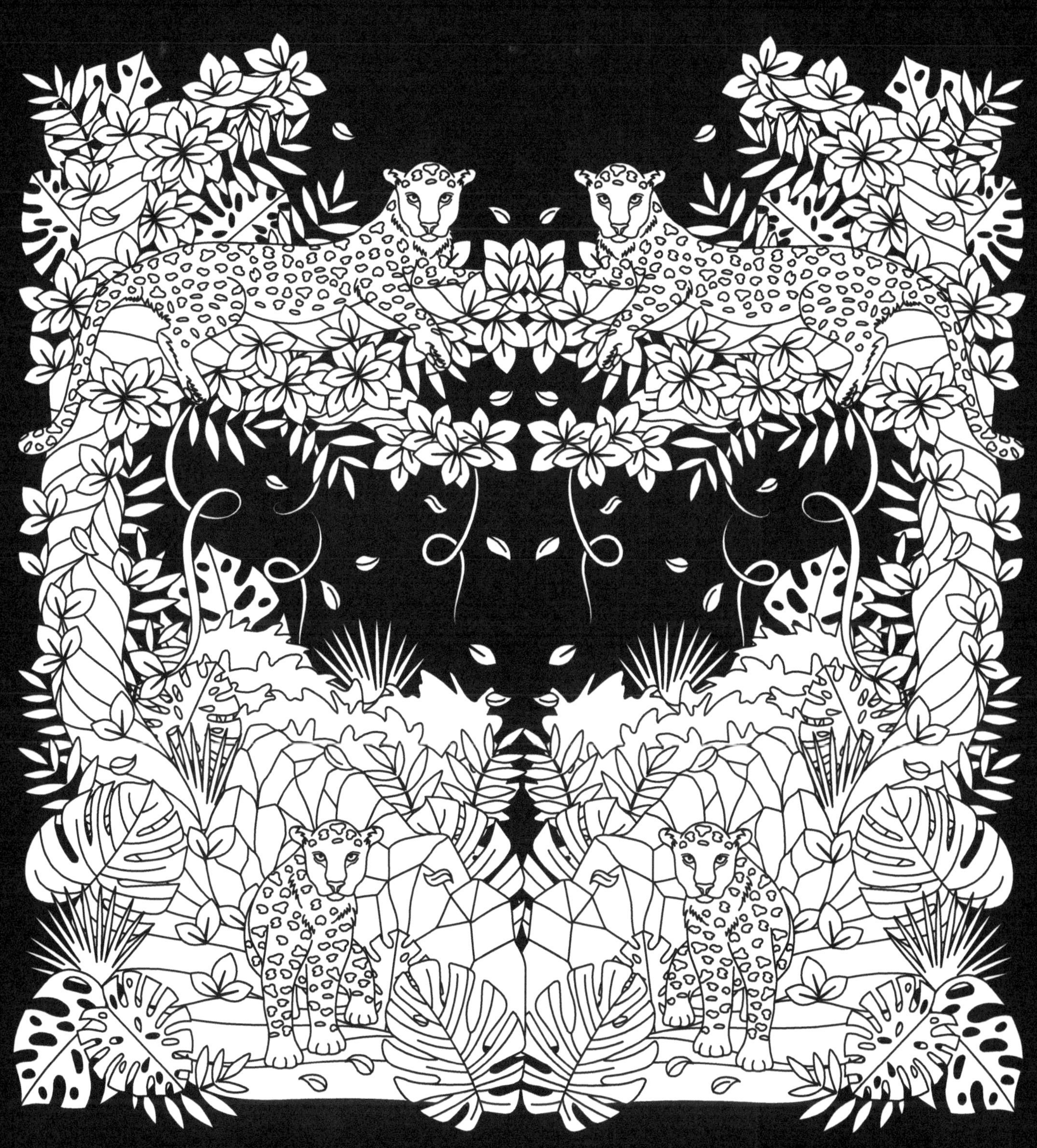

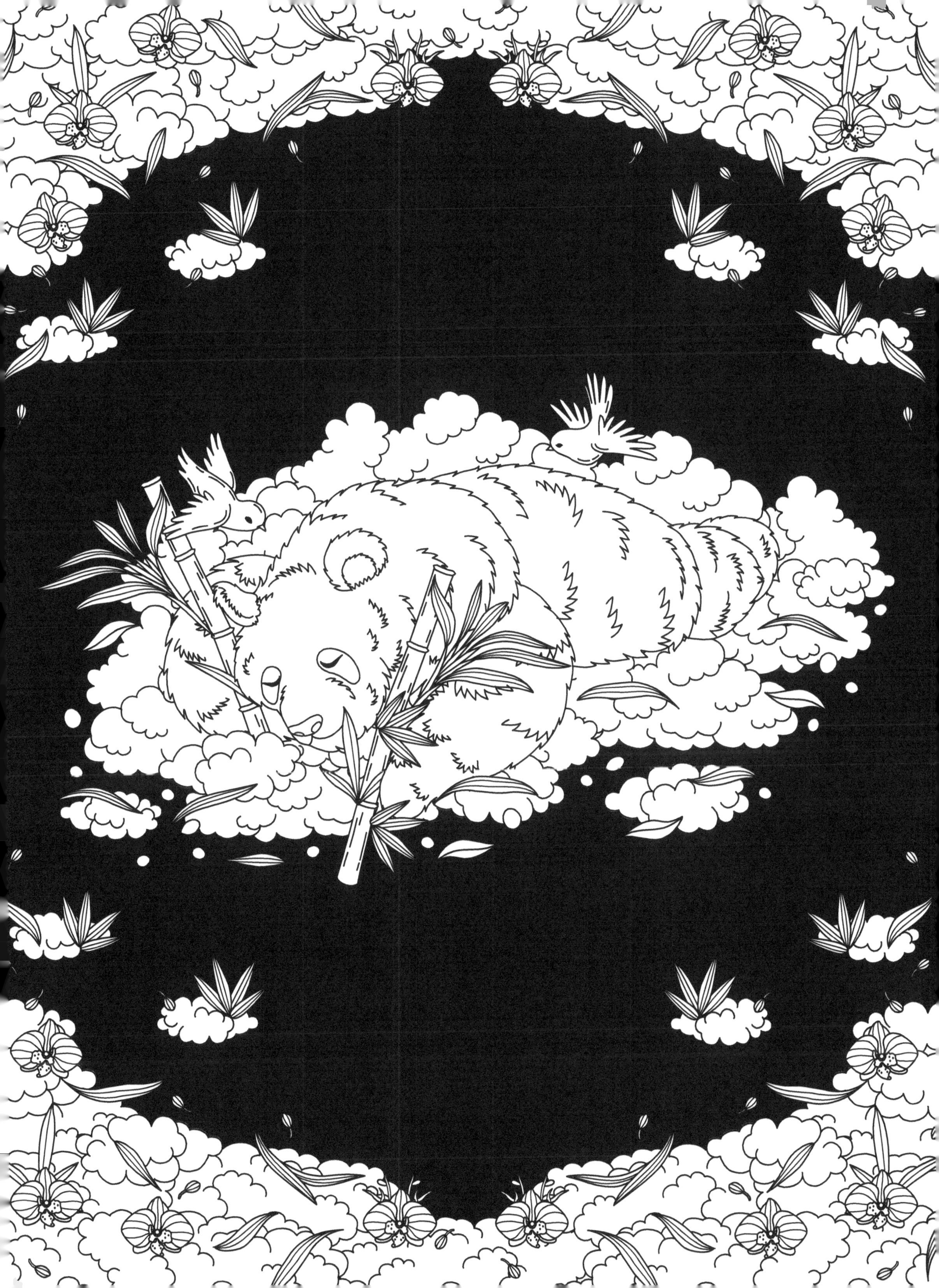

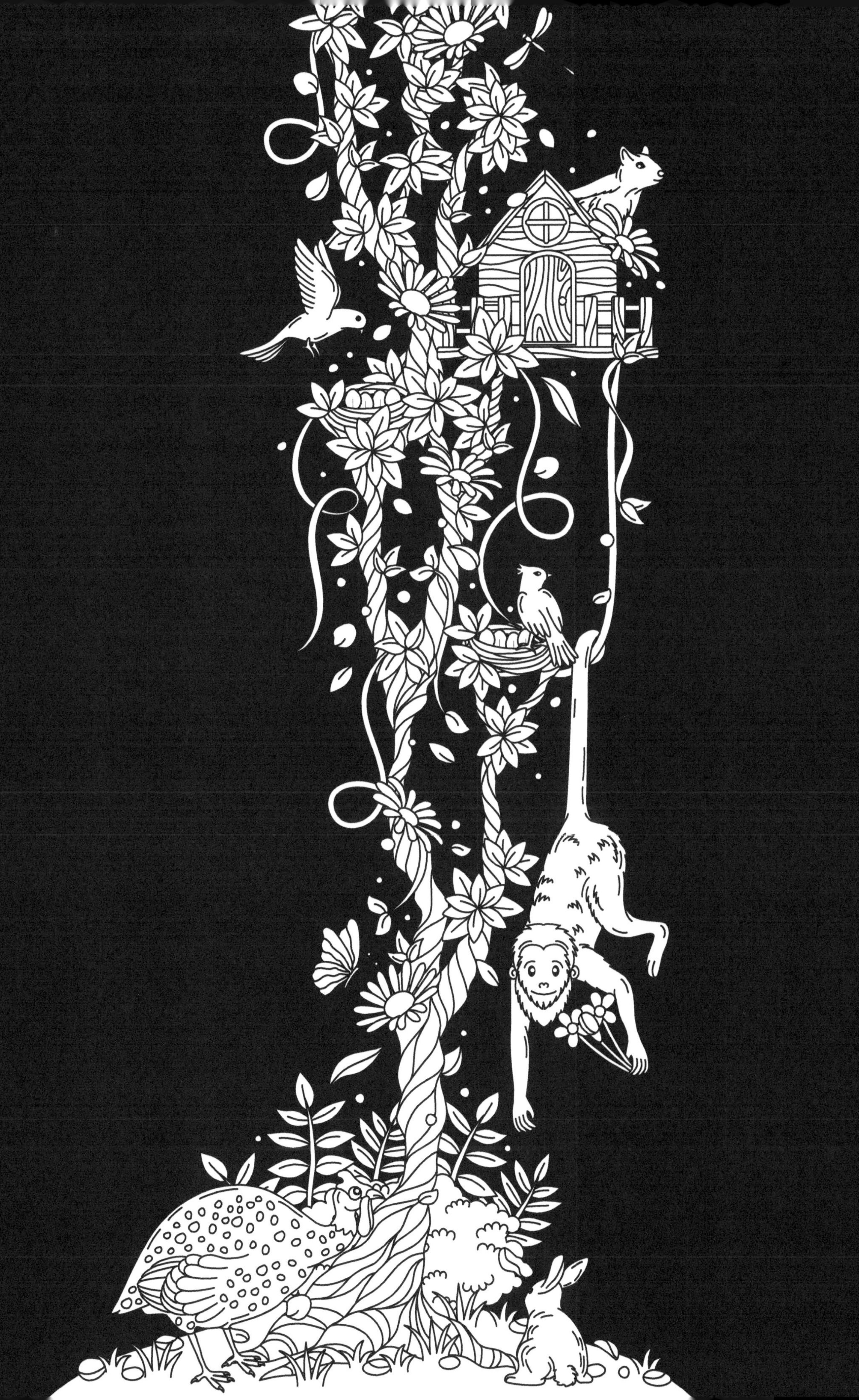

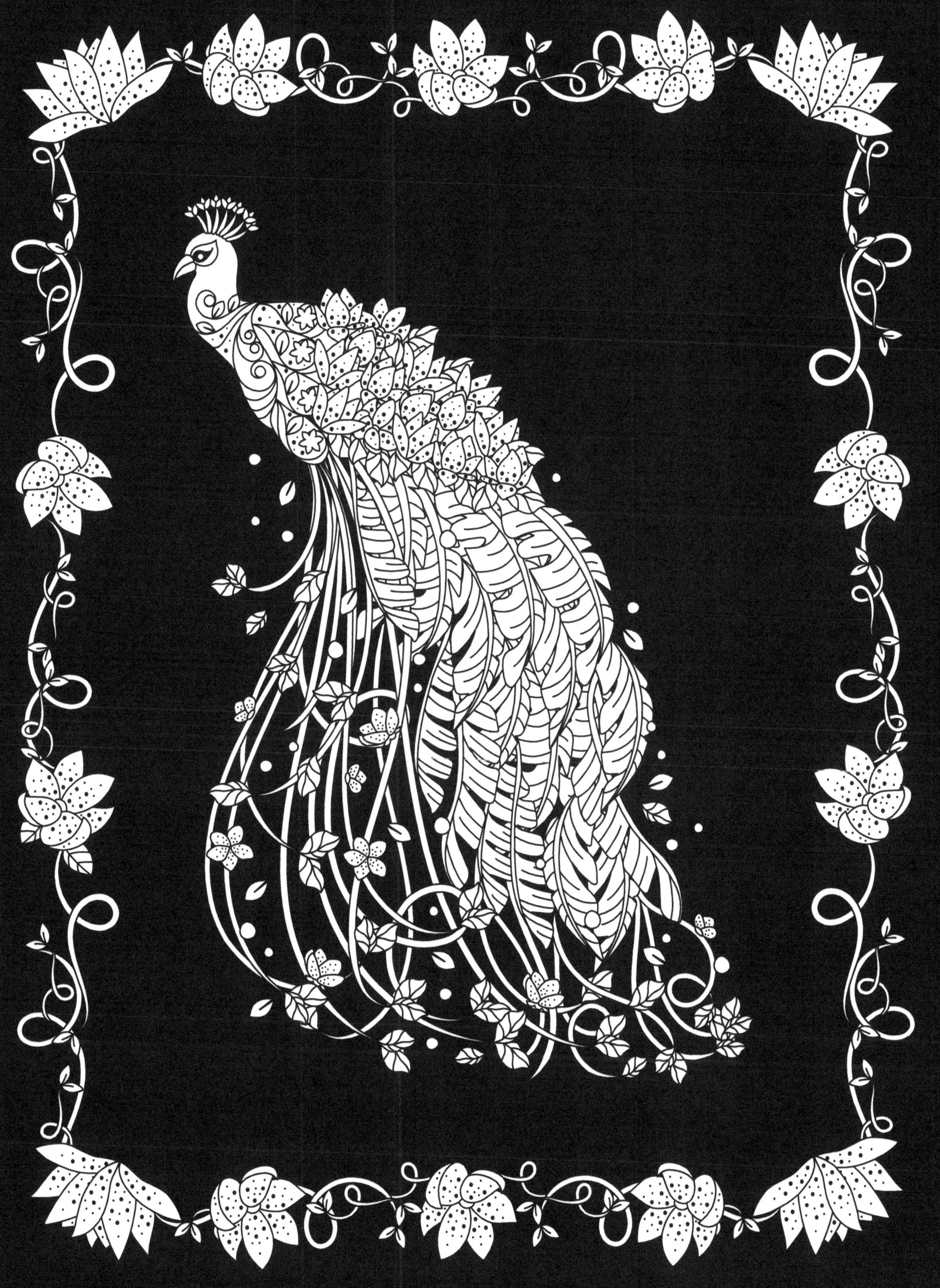

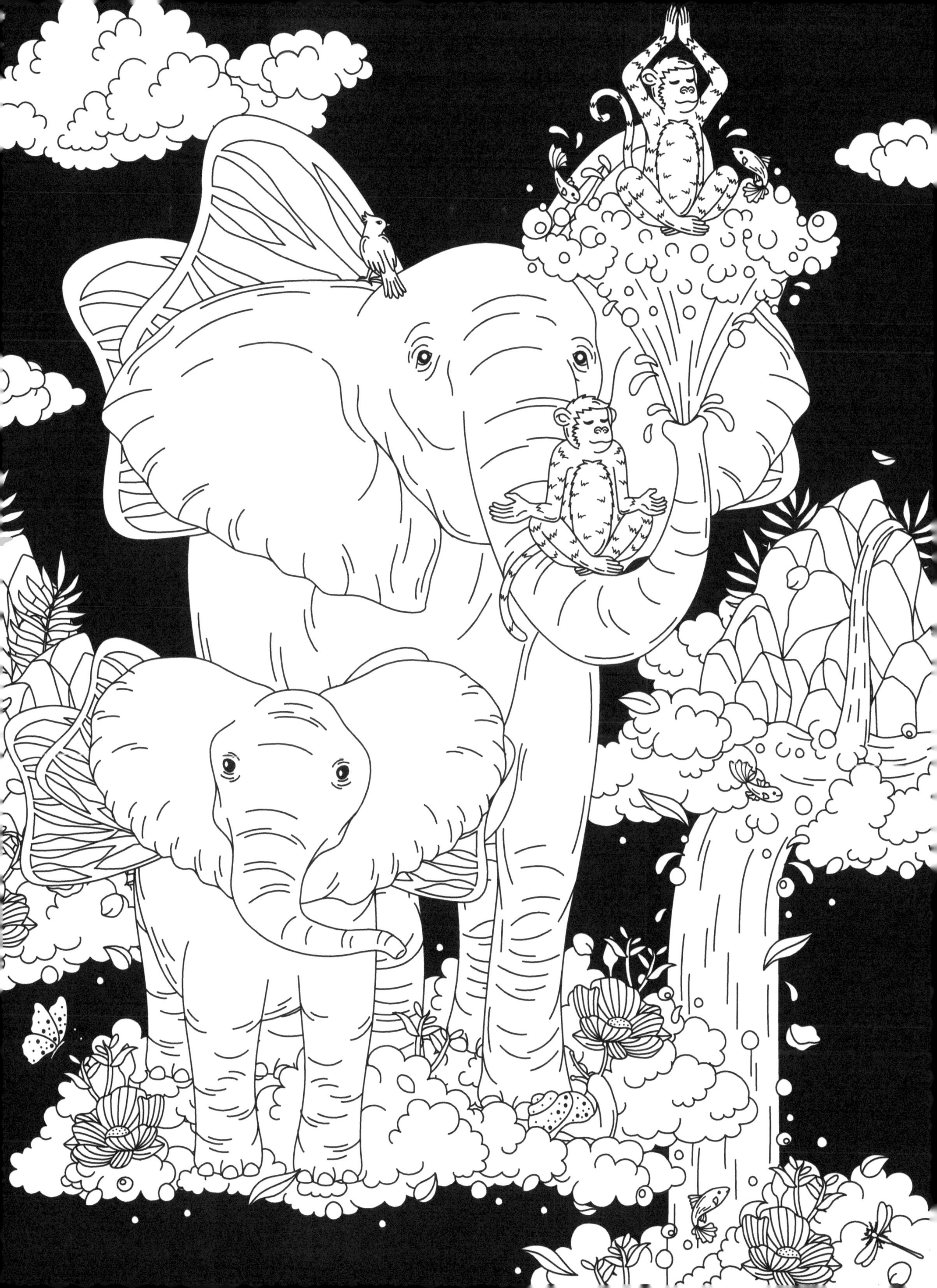

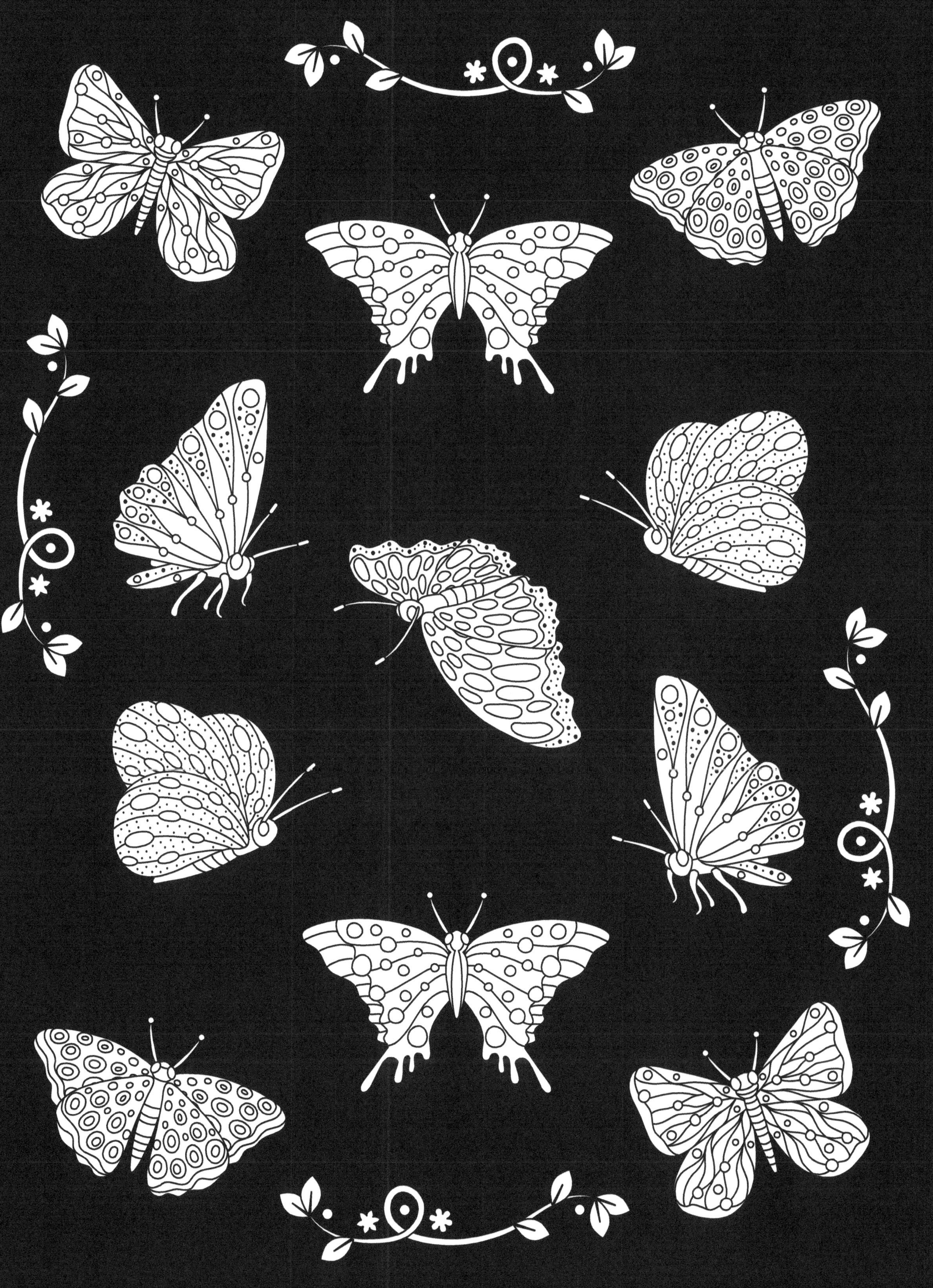

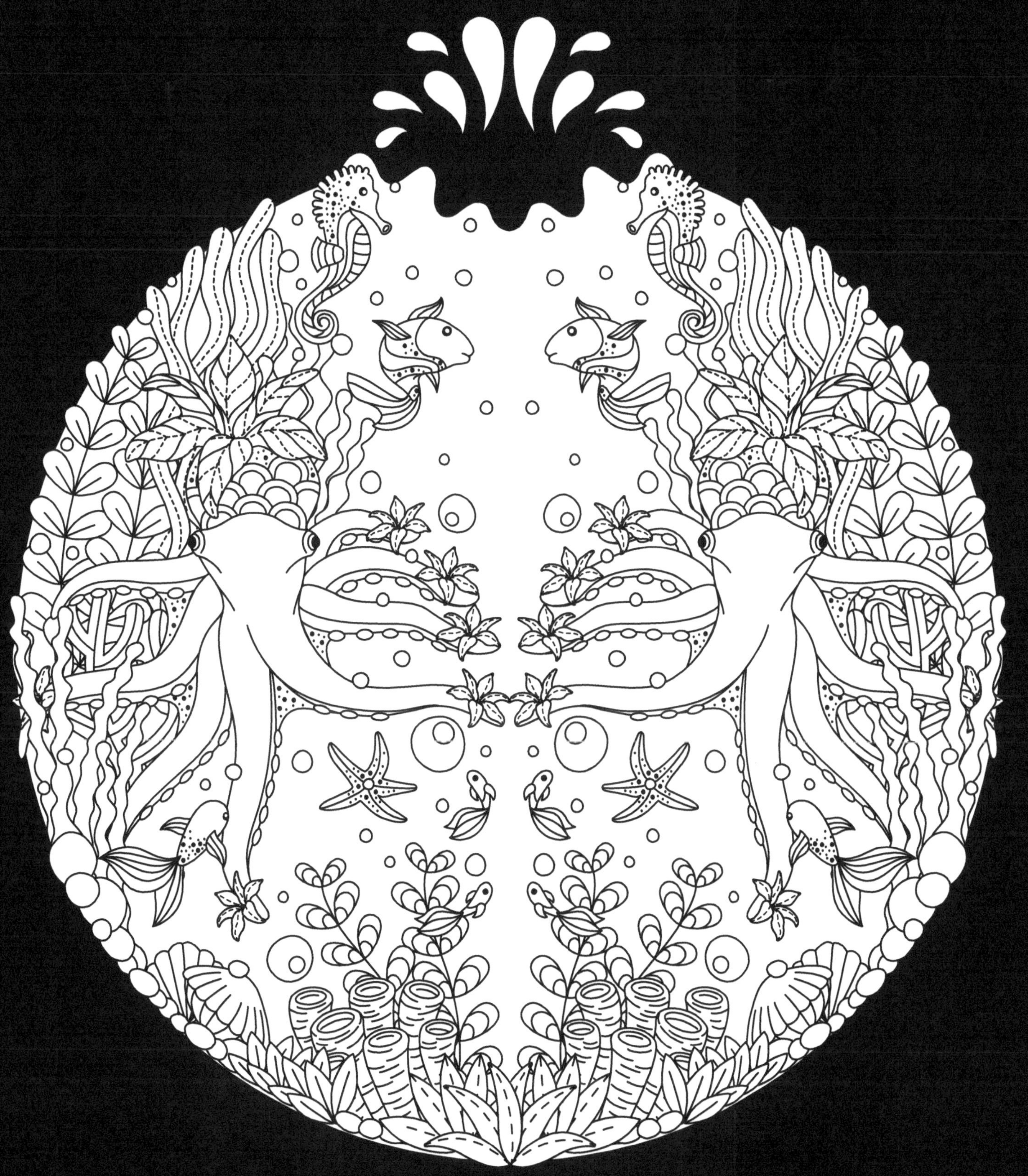

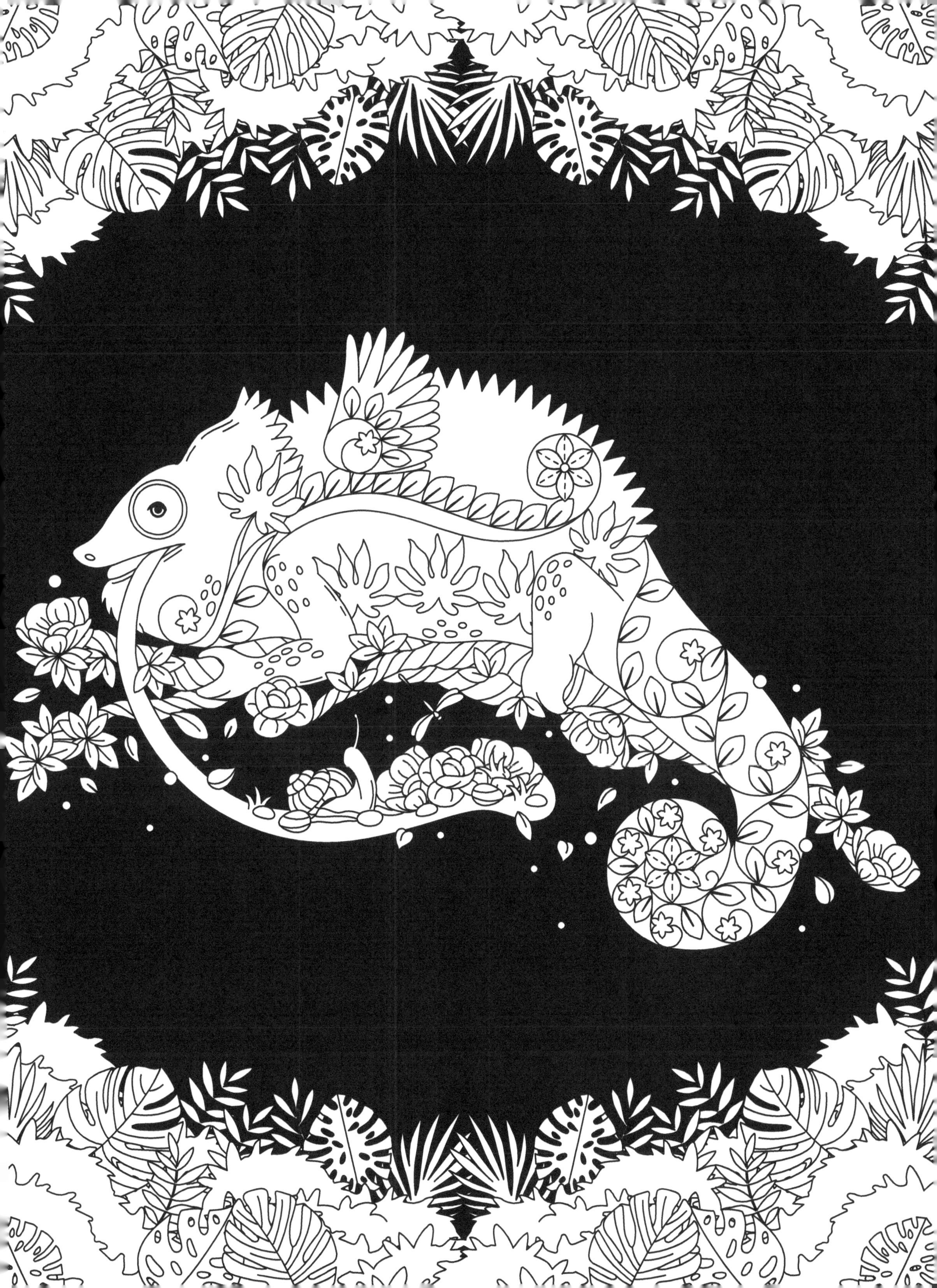

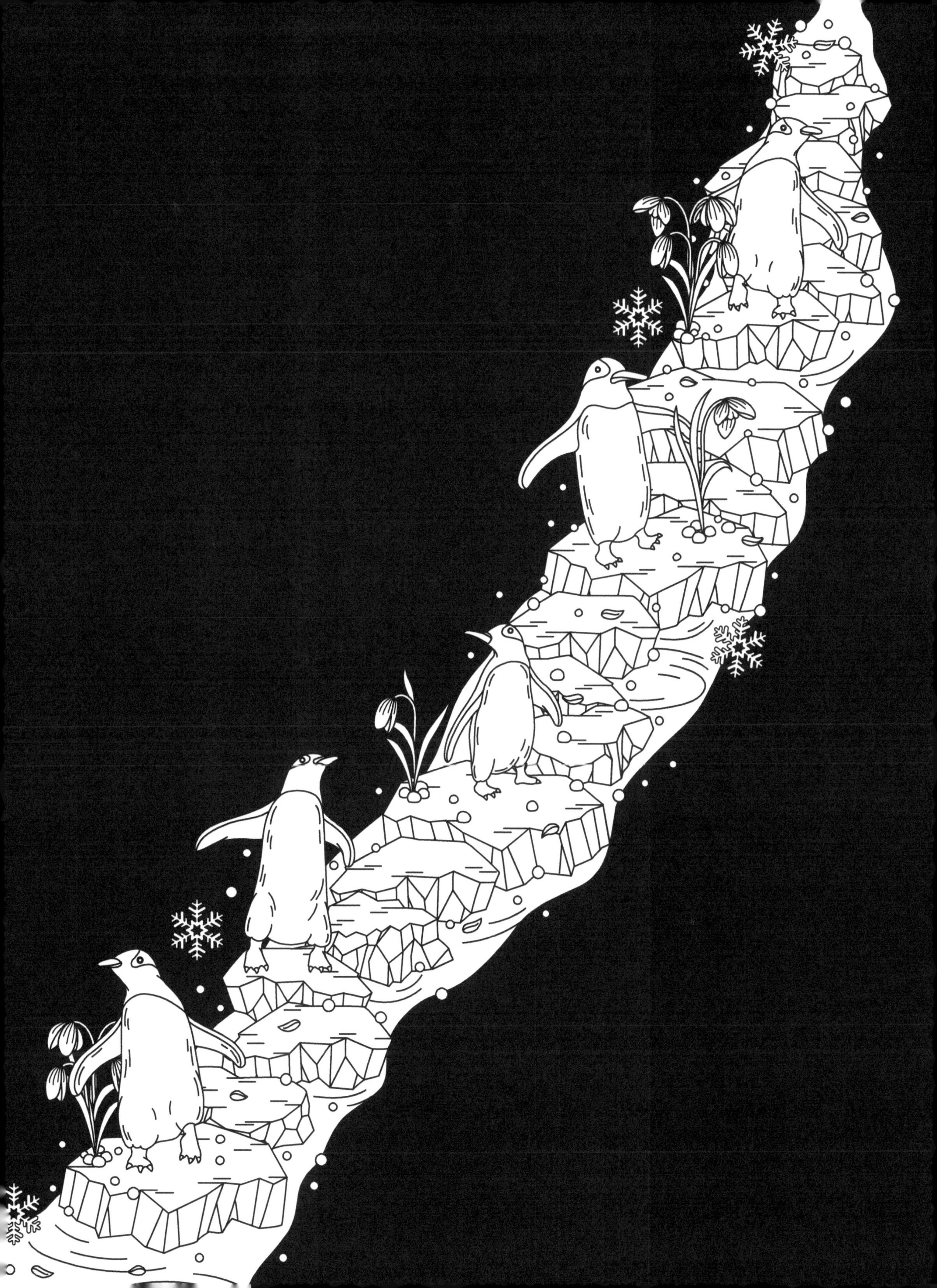

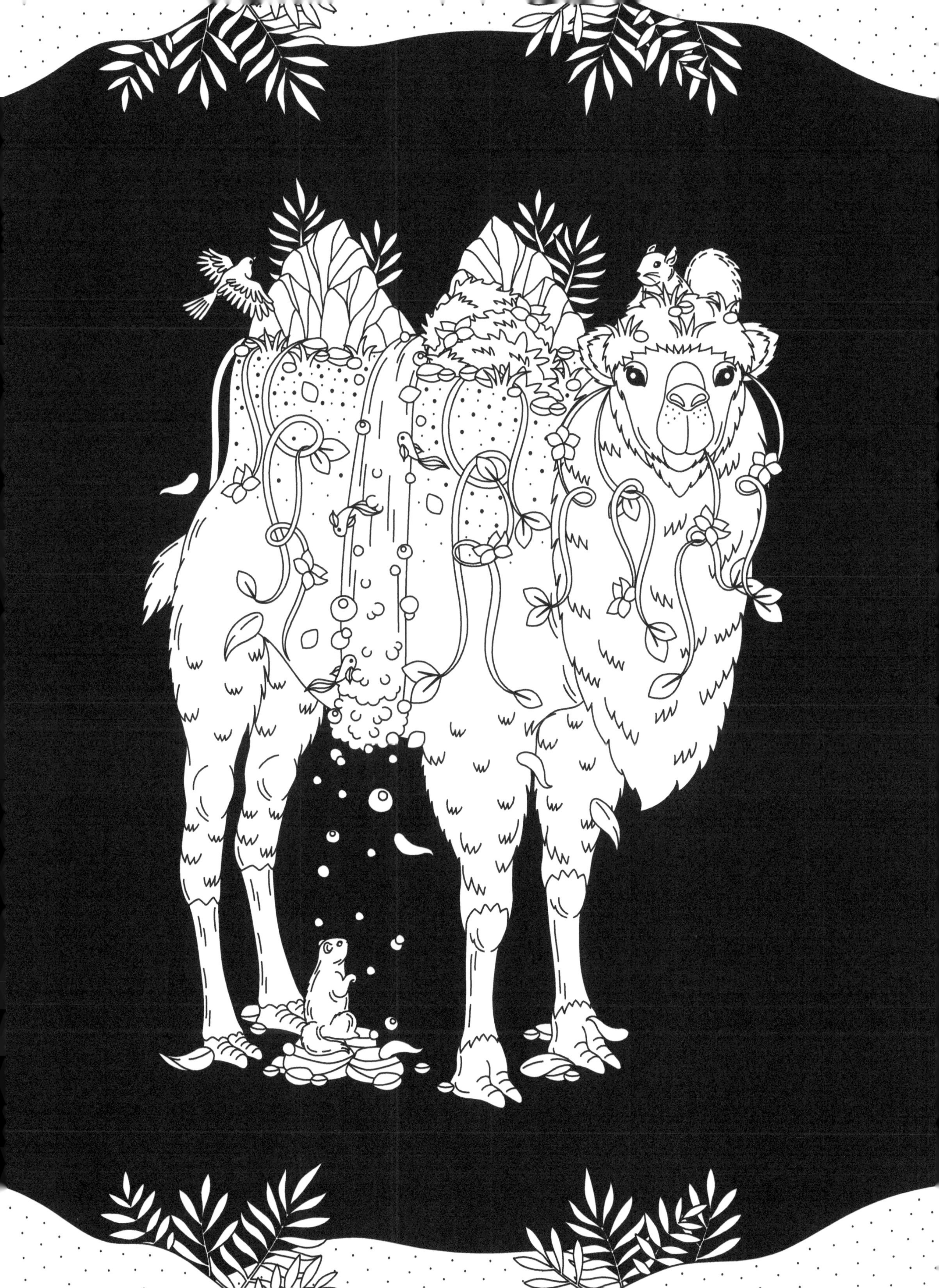

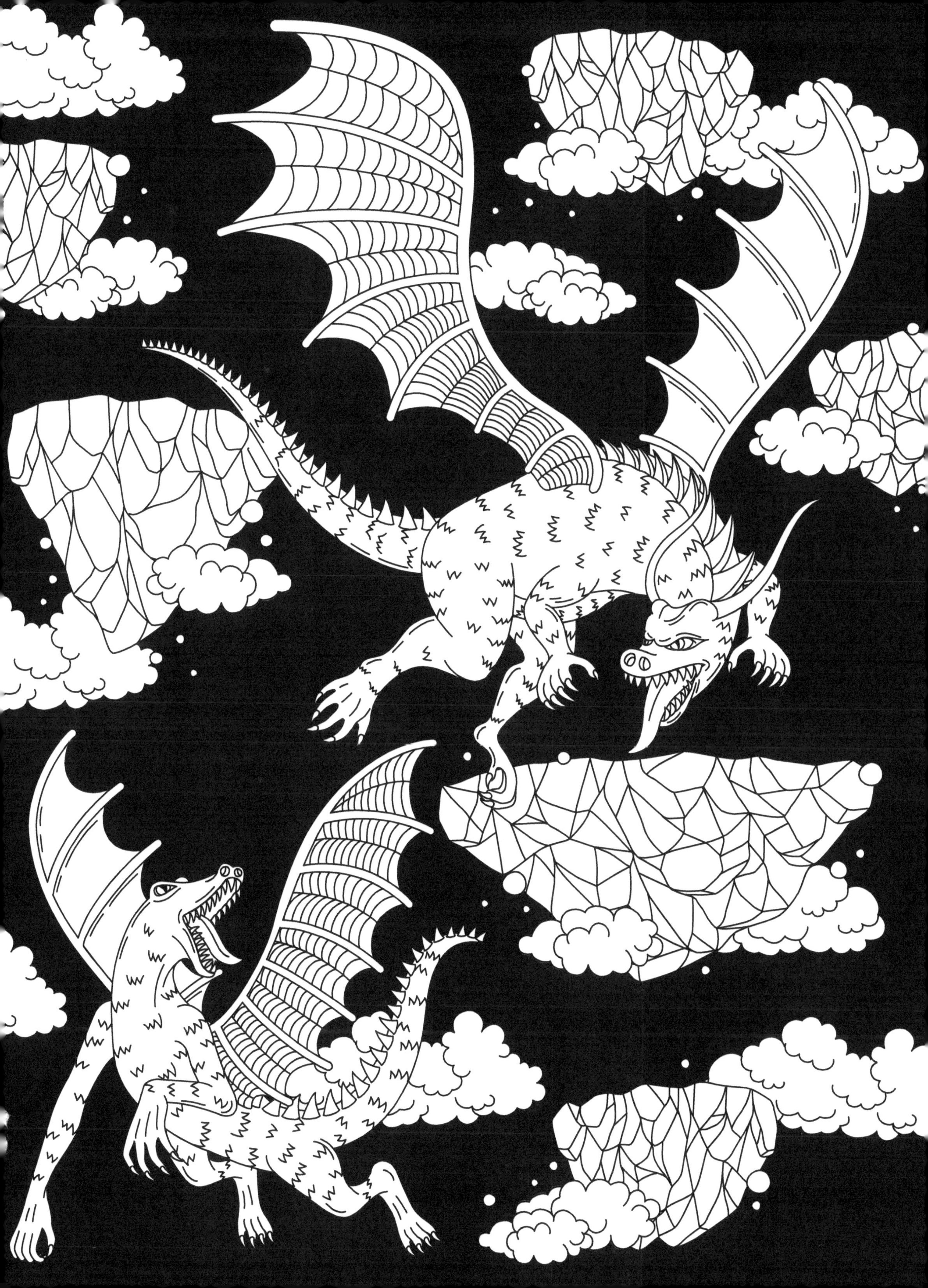

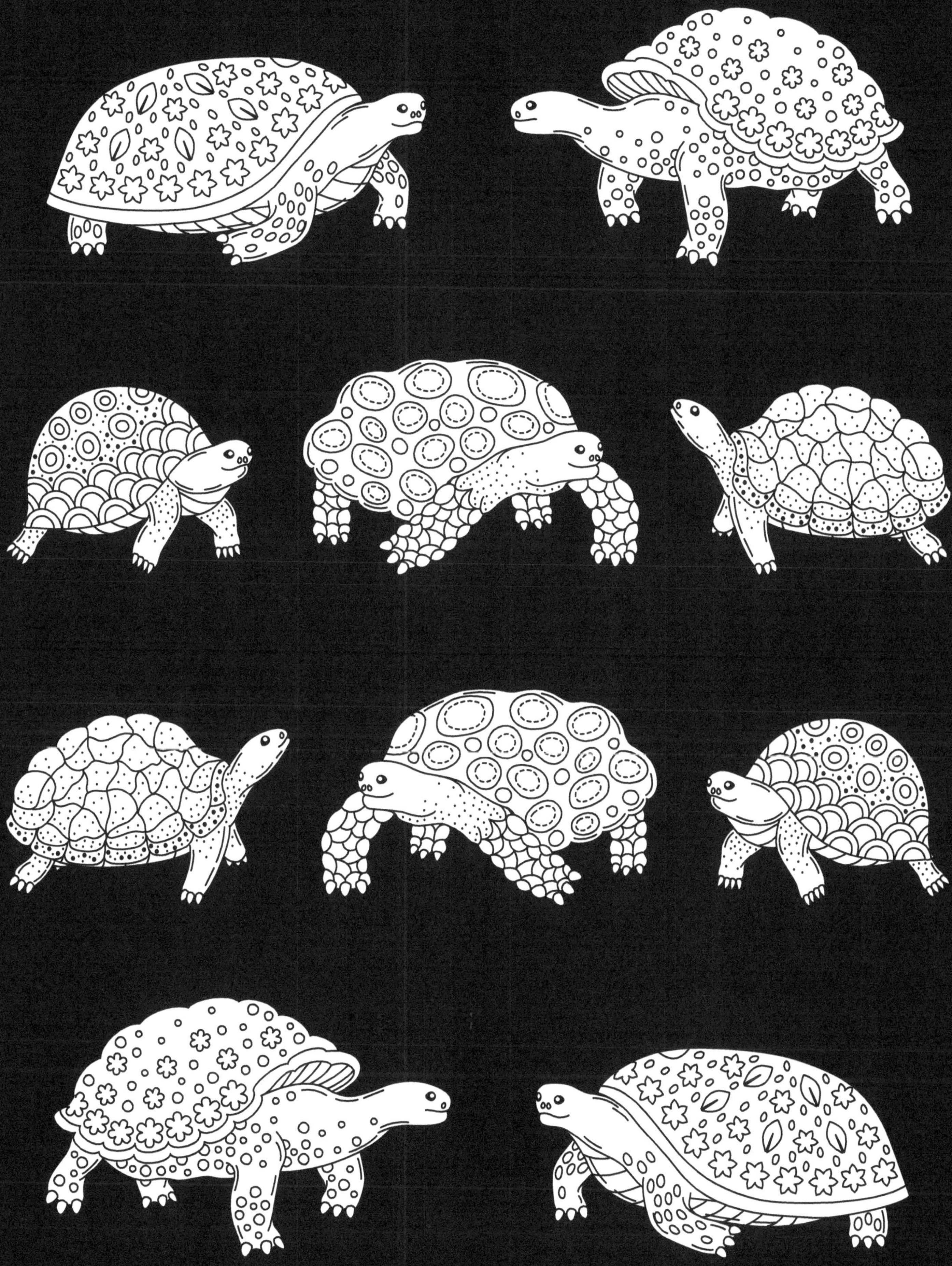

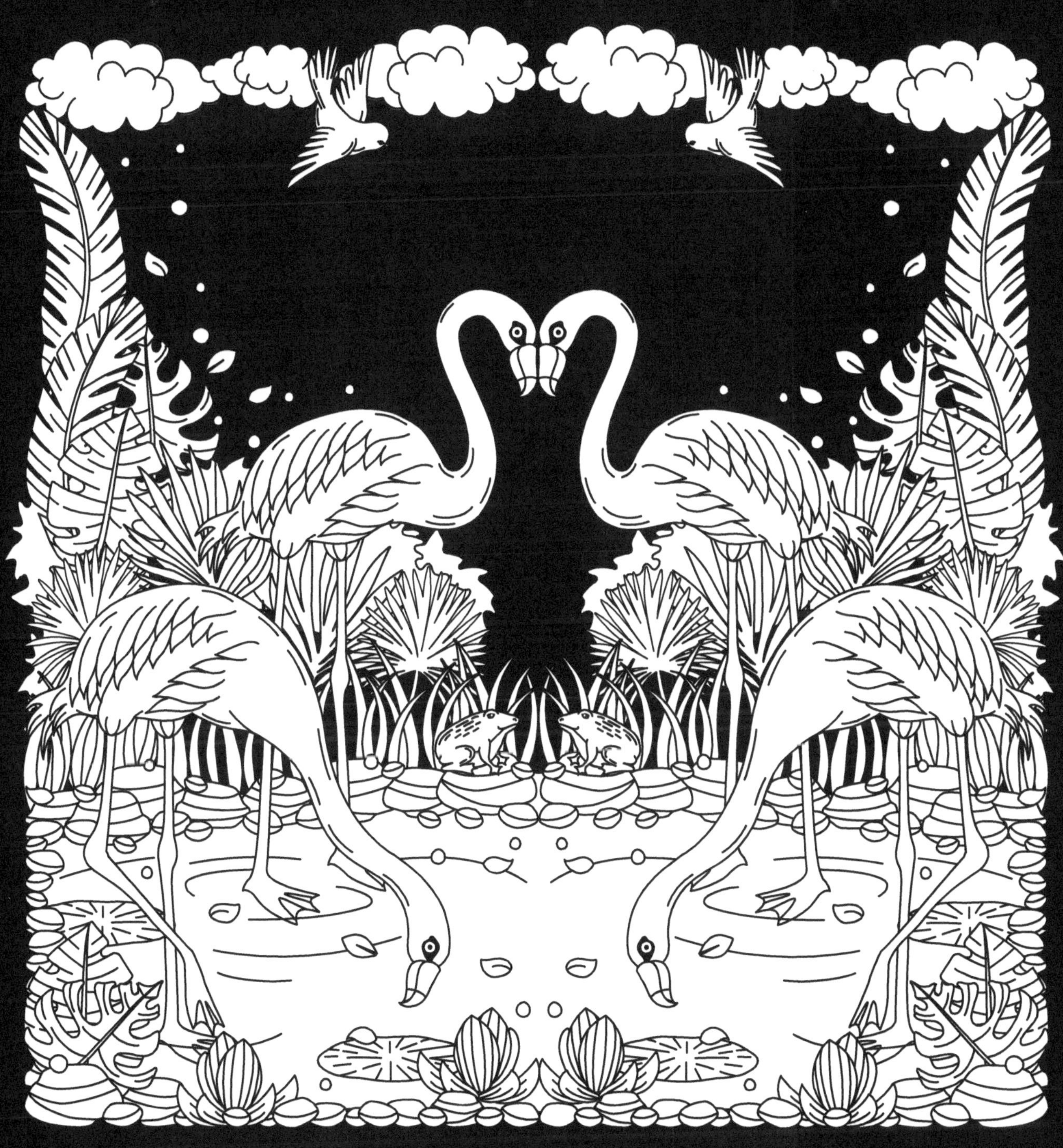

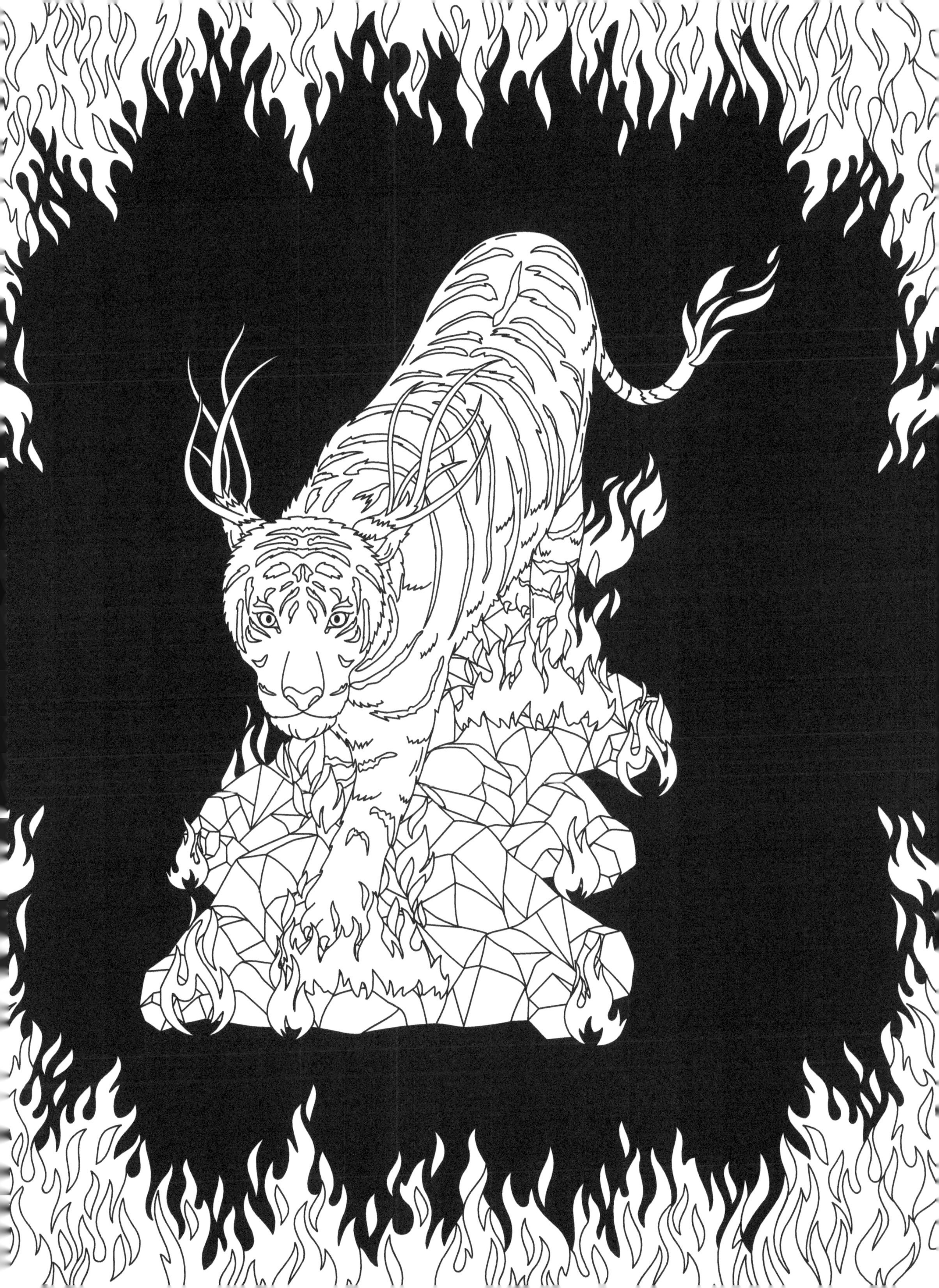

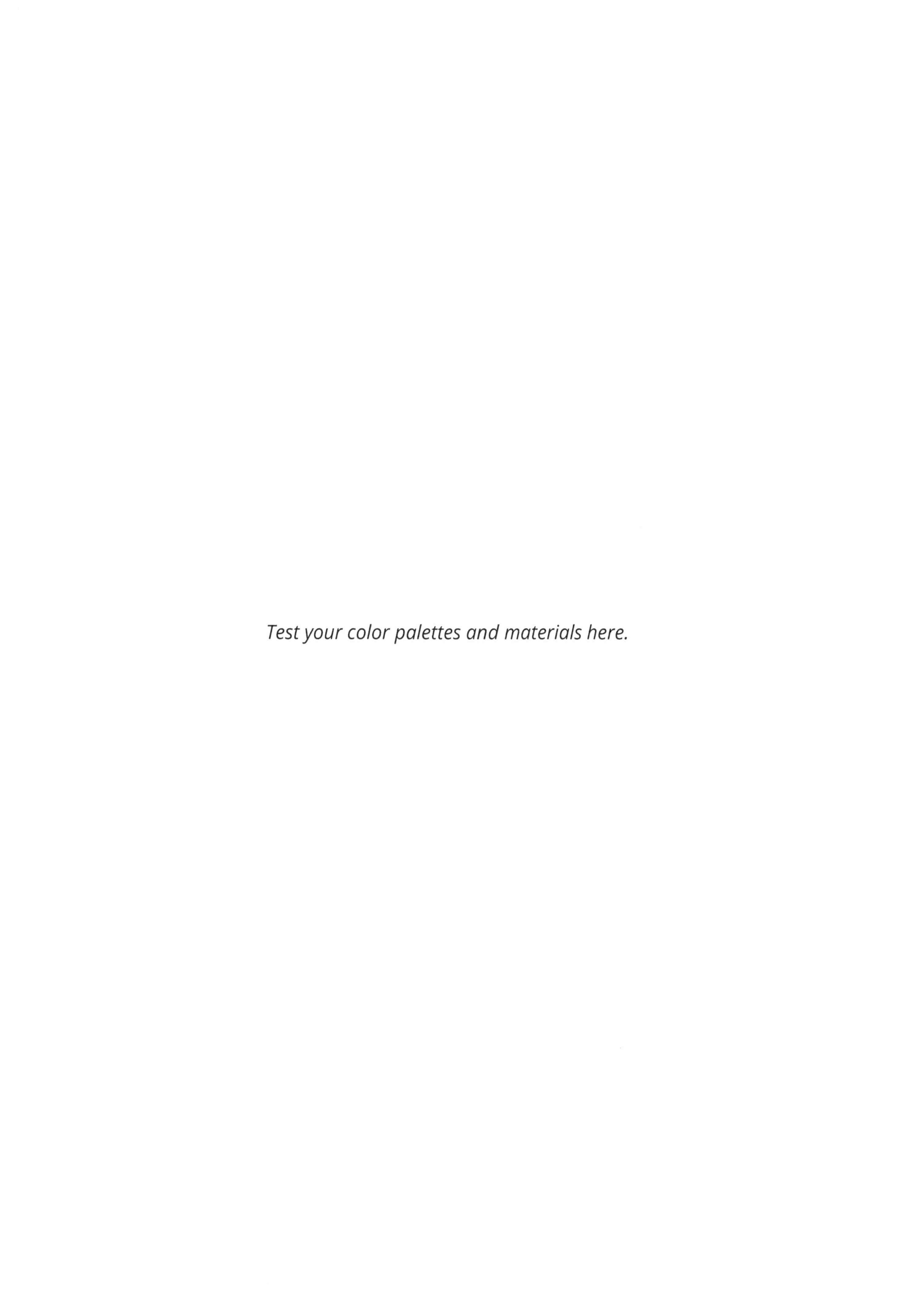
Test your color palettes and materials here.

*There are no rules when it comes to coloring – go wild
and be as creative as you like!*

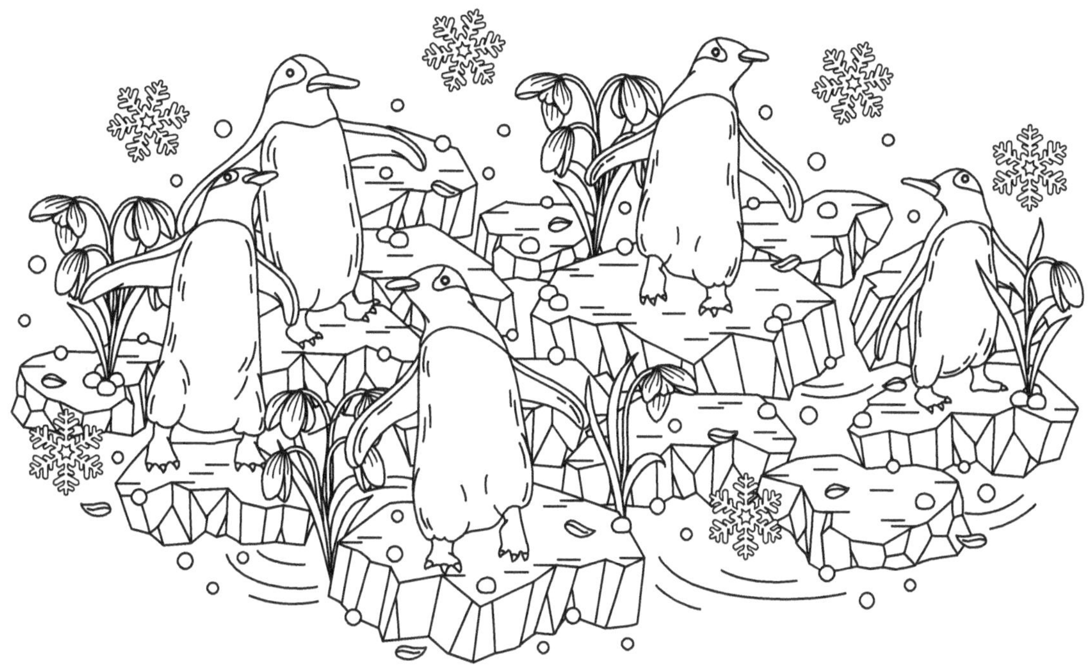

Thank you for purchasing Remarkable Creatures. Your feedback will help us create better quality coloring books, and it will also help others make more informed decisions.

To leave a review on Amazon, search for Remarkable Creatures by Runny Rainbows, check your recent orders, or scan the QR code below for the direct link to leave a review.

Also from Runny Rainbows

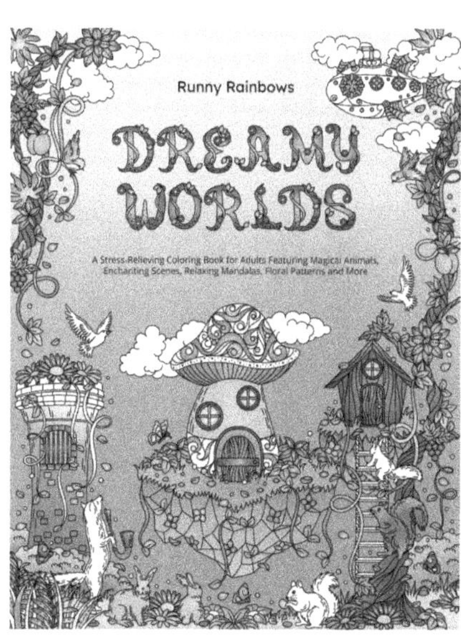
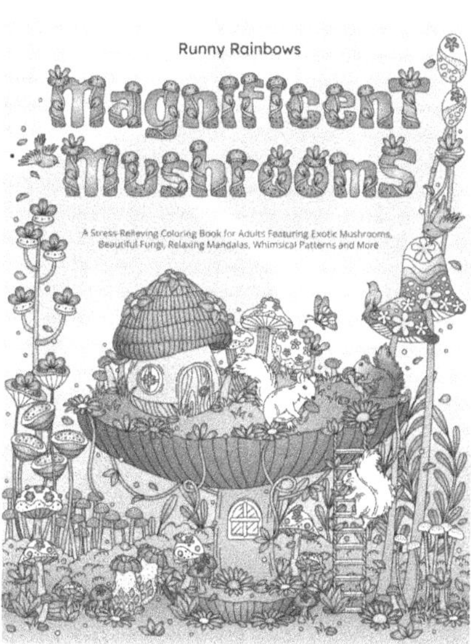
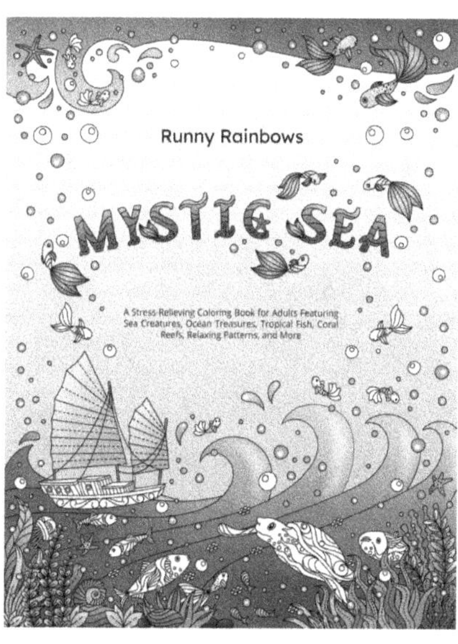